PHILOLOGY OF THE GOSPELS.

PHILOLOGY
OF THE GOSPELS.

BY

FRIEDRICH BLASS, Dr.Phil.,
D.Th., Hon. LL.D., Dublin,

PROFESSOR OF CLASSICAL PHILOLOGY IN THE
UNIVERSITY OF HALLE-WITTENBERG.

AMSTERDAM
B. R. GRÜNER - PUBLISHER
1969

UNCHANGED REPRINT OF THE
EDITION LONDEN 1898

CONTENTS.

CONTENTS.

CHAPTER VII.

CHAPTER VIII.

CHAPTER IX.

CHAPTER X.

CHAPTER XI.

CHAPTER XII.

INDICES.

PREFACE.

THE present book is due to the initiative of my friend Prof. J. P. Mahaffy, who proposed to Messrs. Macmillan that they should ask me to write it. Prof. Mahaffy and Mr. George Macmillan revised either the manuscript or the proof-sheets, and the MS. had been previously submitted to four young American friends of mine, namely, Dr. J. Carter, of New-York, Mr. Charles Downing, of Clinton, Mr. W. Prentice, of New-York, and Mr. H. Sill, of New-York.

F. BLASS.

HALLE, *March,* 1898.

CHAPTER I.

ST. LUKE'S GOSPEL DISTINCTLY A LITERARY WORK.

ANY disquisition concerning the origin and connection of the four Gospels containing the life and teaching of our Lord ought to start from the Gospel of St. Luke, although it confessedly is not the first written Gospel, perhaps not even the earliest of the extant Gospels. The reason is, that only this one is a literary production in the stricter sense of the word, opening with an elaborate dedication like other literary productions of that age, as also of our own. A shorter form of dedication appears in the continuation or second part of Luke's work, viz., in the Acts, the preface or proem being replaced by a simple address to the person to whom both the first and second parts are inscribed. Now, we may easily find plenty of similar instances in Greek and Roman authors, not indeed in the very largest works, which, whilst they usually have a long proem, are addressed to general readers, but in those on a smaller scale, or in those divided into separate parts, like the Biographies of Plutarch. This celebrated and well-known work has neither a proper beginning nor a definite close, but seems to have been an unconnected series of pairs of biographies dedicated to a certain Roman grandee of the name of Sossius Senecio. The Biography of Theseus, which is the first one in our editions, although by no means the first written, begins with a long proem justifying the undertaking of this biography and of the comparison between these two men (Theseus and Romulus); the address: Sossius Senecio, is put immediately after the first words, and so it is in other cases where the original beginning has been preserved intact. In other works of literature or science we have prefatory epistles, an even more developed form of dedication than in the case of St. Luke's Gospel. The two first books of the celebrated *Conica* of Apollonius are inscribed in this way to a certain Eudemus, the fourth to a certain Attalus.

But the most noteworthy instance to be compared with St. Luke's Gospel seems to be a medical work. One of our best Orientalists, the late Professor Paul de Lagarde, has written a short note on the proem of Dioscorides in comparison with that of Luke, in order to show nothing less than that Luke has modelled his own proem on that of the well-known author on medical plants.[1] As a philologist, Professor de

---

[1] Paul de Lagarde in *Psalterium juxta hebr. Hieronymi*, p. 165 i.

Lagarde does not entertain so many theological doubts as others on St. Luke's authorship, nor on his being identical with "Lucas the Physician," mentioned by St. Paul (Col. iv. 14); he suggests, therefore, in support of this identity, that Luke was in possession of some medical works, especially of the *Materia Medica* by Dioscorides, who was a native of Cilicia (whilst Luke himself was of the neighbouring Antioch), and, moreover, was at that time a quite recent author. He proceeds next to compare the two proems, and finds that Dioscorides' proem is the model, and Luke's the copy, and not even a good copy. At this point our doubts begin. The main sentence in Dioscorides' proem is this: "Since others have written on the same matter badly, I shall try to write on it better"; whilst Luke says: "Since others have written on the same matter, I, too, may do it." The train of thought therefore is quite different in the two proems: why, then, should there be imitation on the one part? You will say, because the words agree, and that agreement cannot be explained otherwise. But in reality not even the words are the same, except the first in Dioscorides ($\pi o\lambda\lambda\hat{\omega}\nu$), which is (in a different inflexion, however) the second in Luke; and, if we look a little further on, we may find in the medical author (on page 2) such striking test-words as $\pi\alpha\rho\alpha\delta\iota\delta\acute{o}\nu\alpha\iota$ and $\dot{\alpha}\kappa\rho\iota\beta\acute{\epsilon}\sigma\tau\epsilon\rho o\nu$, which are employed similarly, although not identically, by Luke. So I again ask: Why should there be

imitation on Luke's part? Because, says de Lagarde,
the argumentation goes the wrong way: if many had
already done it, then there was no need for a fresh
author, but Luke might refer Theophilus to the books
of the eye-witnesses (αὐτόπται), which were much
more trustworthy than his own could possibly be.
Here is, indeed, a strange mistake on the part of
the learned writer: the eye-witnesses of whom Luke
speaks had not written any books at all, and it
merely marks the modesty of our author that he
does not choose to disparage his predecessors, but only
asserts of himself that he has got very full information,
which is, I should think, a quite sufficient reason
for writing.   There is another still: Theophilus, whom
he addresses, is evidently supposed not to possess any
of the books formerly written.   Now, Luke might
send him these; but possibly they were not even.
written in Greek, but in Aramaic; and, besides, they
did not contain so much information as Luke himself
could give; so he prefers to write a new book.   The
result is that we must, with regret perhaps, dismiss
the ingeniously contrived argument for the author's
identity with "Lucas the Physician," and rely on the
old ones, which are indeed, in my opinion, quite worth
relying on.

We might at once go on to examine the rest of
this interesting proem, but we are still detained by
the address we were speaking of.   A literary work

which is, like this, inscribed to a definite person
cannot come from an indefinite author, but must have
borne from the first a distinct author's name. We
are not bound to inquire whether this rule holds
good for all modern works without exception, since
it does for all ancient ones as far as we know. But
in what way would the name of the author come in?
An author might indeed begin with his own name,
either like Herodotus and Thucydides, in whose works
the first sentences are very like an enlarged title,
or, in a more modern way, by prefacing his work
with a dedicatory epistle, the inscription of which,
according to the Greek and Roman style, must run
thus : " N. N. to N. N. greeting." As we find
neither in Luke, nor in Dioscorides, nor in many
other writings, such an epistle, the only place left
for recording the author's name was the title of the
book. Long ago the title had got a separate and
independent existence, and for this same reason was
liable to get lost, as it is lost in Luke's case. The
title of the Gospel was approximately : Λουκᾶ ᾿Αντιο-
χέως πρὸς Θεόφιλον λόγος πρῶτος, and of the Acts
Λ. ᾿Α. πρὸς Θ. λ. δεύτερος. No extant manuscript
gives these titles, because St. Luke's works had been
merged into the collection of sacred books of the
Christian Church, and especially his Gospel into the
collection of canonical Gospels, whose inscriptions run
all in the same strain : " According to Matthew, Mark,

Luke, John." If there had been selected but one
canonical Gospel, even these distinctions would have
disappeared, as they have in the case of the Marcionite
canon. Because Marcion recognized but one Gospel,
that of Luke, and but one apostle, namely, St. Paul:
one part of his canon was simply superscribed
Gospel and the other simply Apostle. It has been
wrongly inferred from this inscription "Gospel" that
Luke's name was not known to Marcion; we might
just as well infer from the other inscription that he
did not know the name of Paul. But the case being
that the Church recognized four separate Gospels, the
names of the authors have been preserved, that is
to say, the most valuable part of Luke's original
superscription. We may well ask in what way the
Church got at the three other names; but in Luke's
case it was most easy to pick it up. There are
classical writings whose authors have become unknown
by the loss of the title, as is the case with the well-
known rhetorical treatise on the "Sublime" (wrongly
ascribed to Longinus), which, like Luke's works, is
addressed to a single person (Postumius Terentianus),
and must of course originally have had an author's
name in the title; the Acts also would have become
anonymous, and are really so (the inscription being
simply Πράξεις τῶν ἀποστόλων), but that, with certainty, the first part of the whole work preserved the
author's name.

CHAPTER II.

THE PROEM OF ST. LUKE.

THE proem of Luke's Gospel gives so much valuable information, both on the author's work and on the preceding work of others, that it well deserves a most careful examination, the more so as it has been from very ancient times seriously misunderstood in more than one point. We shall examine it, in the first instance, from the literary point of view, and next with regard to its contents.

The opening sentence of this Gospel is a very remarkable specimen of fine and well-balanced structure, and at the same time of well-chosen vocabulary. It has no parallel, in these respects taken together, either in the Gospel itself or in the Acts; it is unnecessary to add that the other three Gospels are far from exhibiting anything similar. Luke has tried to give to his work (after the Pindaric phrase) a πρόσωπον τηλαυγές, and has succeeded very well. This, too, is an additional proof of the literary character of the

work, in contrast to the writings of the other three.
He employs, in this proem, grander words and better
Greek than he generally does, or than others do;
for he was here free to give a sentence wholly his
own, which did not form a part of the sacred narrative, and would not lose its becoming, simple, dignity
by touches of literary refinement. Of course I cannot
explain this without entering into details which may
seem to us minute and trivial, though they were not
regarded in that light by the ancients. The very first
word is ἐπειδήπερ, never occurring again in the New
Testament; it was evidently employed instead of
ἐπειδή on account of its length and grandeur. Then
comes πεπληροφορημένων, instead of which he might
have written πληρωθέντων, which gives the same sense
(on which we shall speak below); but again the former
was grander and more sonorous. The first word in
verse 2 is in the common text καθώς, but the Cambridge codex, which will occupy us more hereafter,
and two quotations in Eusebius[1] give, instead of this
καθώς, the apparently identical καθά. What is the
difference? Simply this, that καθώς is vulgar, and
καθά is Attic. As a native of Antioch, and of Greek
(or Hellenized) extraction, Luke had necessarily undergone discipline from a grammarian, and that grammarian had taught him: Do not write καθώς, for
that word has no classic authority; but write καθό,

---

[1] Euseb. *Hist. Eccl.* iii. 4. 6; *Demonstr. Evang.*, p. 120.

which has the authority of Thucydides, or καθά which
is equally good.[1]   Luke's days were those of reigning
Atticism, the general tendency of the literary world
being to look backwards to the classic period of the
language and literature, when both language and taste
were pure and not infected by barbarous influences,
which had, from Alexander's time, substituted in
literature the taste and style of Caria and Phrygia
for that of Athens.   St. Paul, too, when he was
called to speak before King Agrippa, and Queen
Berenice, and the Praeses (or Procurator) Festus, and
the most distinguished society of Caesarea and of
the whole province, took care (if we trust, as we
ought to do, Luke's account in Acts xxvi.) not
to employ vulgar inflections of the verbs, but to say
ἴσασιν πάντες Ἰουδαῖοι, not οἴδασιν.   In his epistles,
he constantly has οἴδαμεν, -ατε, -ασιν; but his
schoolmaster at Tarsus had warned him against such
vulgarisms : " ἴσμεν, ἴστε, ἴσασιν," he must have said,
" are the true forms which you must employ if you
care to be considered a cultivated speaker or writer."
Likewise in Luke the next word is παρέδοσαν.   The
colloquial forms of the time, and for that reason
those of all New Testament writers, were ἐδώκαμεν,
ἐδώκατε, ἔδωκαν, but schoolmasters (then as now)
drilled their pupils to make use of the correct Attic

[1] Cf. Rutherford, *The New Phrynichus*, p. 495.

forms (although, in this case, the incorrect ones are not altogether alien to Attic poetry, or to Attic prose of the fourth century).

Moreover, it is easy to show that the structure of this opening sentence is extremely well balanced. It consists, as we say, of a protasis and an apodosis, which are pretty nearly equal in length; but according to the rhetorical doctrine of the ancients we may divide it into six members, or *cola*, in this way: Ἐπειδήπερ πολλοὶ ἐπεχείρησαν | ἀνατάξασθαι διήγησιν τῶν πεπληροφορημένων ἐν ἡμῖν πραγμάτων | καθὰ παρέδοσαν ἡμῖν οἱ ἀπ' ἀρχῆς αὐτόπται καὶ ὑπηρέται γενόμενοι τοῦ λόγου || ἔδοξε κἀμοὶ παρηκολουθηκότι ἄνωθεν πᾶσιν ἀκριβῶς | καθεξῆς σοι γράψαι κράτιστε Θεόφιλε | ἵνα ἐπιγνῷς περὶ ὧν κατηχήθης λόγων τὴν ἀσφάλειαν. Three of these members belong to the protasis, three to the apodosis; the sense of each of the former members stands in corresponding relation to the sense of the latter, inasmuch as πολλοὶ stands in opposition to κἀμοὶ, ἀνατάξασθαι διήγησιν is parallel to γράψαι κ.τ.λ.; and, lastly, the tradition of the eye-witnesses, which is treated in the third member, is again referred to in the sixth with its ἀσφάλειαν. There is even an opposition between παρέδοσαν (3), and κατηχήθης (6); but of this we must speak hereafter, as it belongs to the interpretation of the proem. Our author abandons this elaborate style suddenly, abruptly, the very first words of the following narrative being not original Greek, but transparent Hebrew, and he never returns to his first style, not even in the beginning of the Acts, which was modelled, as it seems, on the beginning of the corresponding second part of one of Luke's authorities.

I may add that there has been preserved a much shorter form of the same proem, probably, or possibly, belonging to a second edition, or, to speak more correctly, to a second authentic copy of Luke's Gospel, where the dedication to Theophilus had been suppressed. A contemporary of Chrysostom, Severianus, bishop of Gabala in Syria, some of whose sermons have been preserved among those of Chrysostom, gives a comparison between the beginnings of the four Gospels, and states that of Luke in this form: Ἐπειδήπερ πολλοὶ . . . πραγμάτων, ἔδοξε κἀμοὶ παρηκολουθηκότι τοῖς πᾶσιν ἀπ' ἀρχῆς γράψαι, καθὼς παρέδοσαν ἡμῖν οἱ ἀπ' ἀρχῆς αὐτόπται καὶ ὑπηρέται γενόμενοι τοῦ λόγου.[1] Here the six members have been reduced to four, by leaving out the sixth, and retaining of the fifth nothing but

[1] Chrysost. opp. Vol. xii. 567. The editions give not παρηκολουθηκότι but παρακολουθηκότι, and the editors record παρακολουθῆσαι as a various reading in the mss. If we adopt this reading, we must of course strike out γράψαι, which might indeed be dispensed with.

γράψαι (which cannot form a member by itself);
but in order not to destroy the balance between the
protasis and the apodosis, the third member has
been (quite neatly) transposed from the former into
the latter.

Now, what is the meaning of the proem? and
what is the true translation? The latter question
is by no means superfluous, as there have been
many misinterpretations, from very ancient times.
There is no doubt that Hieronymus (Jerome), the
author of the Latin Vulgate, well understood both
the colloquial and the literary Greek of his own
time; but in the course of more than three centuries
the literary language had undergone some change,
and as the proem contains not vulgar but choice
Greek, misunderstandings on the part of a writer so
much later may well be expected. Still Jerome has
understood the proem much more correctly than the
great Eusebius himself, and we must confess that
the author had not sufficiently provided against
misunderstandings, purposing, as we have seen, to
make a πρόσωπον τηλαυγές, by means of words not
vulgar, but grand and sonorous. Jerome's translation
of the first verse runs thus: *Quoniam quidem multi
conati sunt ordinare narrationem quae in nobis completae sunt rerum.* Πεπληροφορημένων = *completae* is
right; ἀνατάξασθαι = *ordinare* is wrong; we shall speak

of the former first. Eusebius in his *History of the Church* (iii. 24. 15) makes the following paraphrase of Luke's words : διήγησιν ποιήσασθαι ὧν αὐτὸς πεπληροφόρητο λόγων, which shows that he took πεπληροφορημένων of conviction and ἐν ἡμῖν of Luke alone : "the things which have been brought to conviction in me." This is strange English, but τῶν πεπληροφορημένων, if it is to have this meaning, is even more strange Greek. Ἡμῖν used of the single person of the speaker, is by no means uncommon in Greek authors, although it is somewhat doubtful whether this idiom extends to New Testament writers ; πληροφορεῖν, "to convince," πεπληροφορημένος, "convinced," is Pauline (*e.g.* Rom. xiv. 5 ; Col. iv. 12) ; but here we have "things convinced," instead of "things existing in the conviction of a person," or "of which that person has been convinced." Would anybody understand "a narrative of the things convinced in me"? We must therefore reject this interpretation, and adopt that of Jerome, who takes πληροφορεῖν like πληροῦν, as we have in Paul (2 Tim. iv. 5, 17), πληροφορεῖν τὴν διακονίαν, πλ. τὸ κήρυγμα in quite the same sense as Luke says (Acts xii. 25), πληρώσαντες τὴν διακονίαν. The editor of Wilke's *Clavis Novi Testamenti*, the Jena professor C. L. W. Grimm, has written a very careful paper on Luke's proem, explaining the

single words and phrases by parallel passages, and
he compares the πεπληροφορημένων with ὡς δ'
ἐπληρώθη ταῦτα in Acts xix. 21.[1] It follows, then,
that ἐν ἡμῖν *in nobis* must be "among us," and the
question arises to whom this "us" may refer. I
confidently answer, to the Christian community
existing in Judaea, most members of which were
a part of that population among which our Lord
had lived and died. The very important fact that
Luke includes himself in that number is to be
discussed later on. We proceed to ἀνατάξασθαι
ordinare (Jerome), which Eusebius renders simply
by ποιήσασθαι. Both the Latin and the Greek
writer confound ἀνατάξασθαι and συντάξασθαι, the
former being apparently unknown to them. Now,
it occurs, as Grimm shows, only twice in the
whole range of Greek literature, once in Plutarch
and once in Irenaeus, besides the passage in question.
Plutarch, in his treatise *De Sollertia Animalium*
(*Moral.* 968 CD), gives a curious narrative of an
elephant, who was rather dull by nature, but at
the same time very eager to learn. This elephant
was being taught some tricks, in which he succeeded
much more poorly than his comrades; but his
ambition made him rise at night and repeat by
himself those movements he was to learn. Now,

[1] See *Jahrbücher für deutsche Theologie*, 1871, p. 38 ff.

this is ἀνατάττεσθαι. The passage runs: ὤφθη νυκτὸς αὐτὸς ἀφ᾽ ἑαυτοῦ πρὸς τὴν σελήνην ἀνατατ-τόμενος τὰ μαθήματα καὶ μελετῶν, "bringing together, repeating from memory," and we see therefore that in this compound the preposition ἀνὰ had by no means lost its sense of repetition. Again, Irenaeus (iii. 21. 2, p. 534, ed. Stieren) gives the well-known Jewish tradition of Ezra's restoring the sacred books of the Old Testament, which had perished by the flames in the capture of Jerusalem. This is expressed by: τοὺς τῶν προγεγονότων προφητῶν πάντας ἀνατάξασθαι λόγους. Here we clearly see the wide difference between συντάξασθαι and ἀνατάξασθαι: what those ancient writers had composed (συνετά-ξαντο) Ezra restored from memory, ἀνετάξατο. Now, is it not indeed strange that Grimm, who gives these two passages as the only instances where this verb occurs, does not come to the conclusion that it must have the same meaning in Luke? As a matter of fact, he identifies, like his predecessors, ἀνατάξασθαι and συντάξασθαι, giving, in this way, one instance among thousands of the enormous power of traditional teaching. In reality, Luke's meaning must be this: "since many writers have undertaken to restore from memory a narrative of the things which have been fulfilled (or have come to pass) among us." Perhaps you will say that any historical

writer writes, in a certain sense, from memory.
But we must look at the next clause : καθὰ παρέδοσαν ἡμῖν οἱ . . . αὐτόπται κ.τ.λ. The thing to
be achieved is the restoration of this παράδοσις,
which of course had been oral, and liable to pass
into oblivion, if it were not in time restored from
living memory. So the use of the verb in Luke is
much like that in Irenaeus, and the attitude and
problem of the earliest Gospel-writers is somewhat
akin to those of Ezra in the legend.

In the second verse : καθὰ παρέδοσαν ἡμῖν οἱ ἀπ᾽
ἀρχῆς αὐτόπται καὶ ὑπηρέται γενόμενοι τοῦ λόγου,
the ἡμῖν recurs, and must of course be taken in the
same sense as before, denoting the Christian Church
of Judaea, which had received the instruction of the
eye-witnesses and first preachers of the "Word," that
is, of the gospel. There is a distinction drawn between the writers (verse 1) and the eye-witnesses,
implying (as I have already observed) that none of
the written Gospels known to the author bore the
name of an apostle; he cannot have known our fourth
Gospel, or the first in any form, and we must suppose
Luke's own work to be earlier than both of these.
The ἀπ᾽ ἀρχῆς cannot refer to the birth of Christ, but
to His baptism only; the passage in Acts i. 21 f.
is decisive in this respect (ἀρξάμενος ἀπὸ τοῦ βαπτί-
σματος Ἰωάνου verse 22), and the beginning of St. Mark

shows that the ordinary narrative of the Gospel started from this point. So far as the apostles were called to be witnesses of the things they had seen and heard, they could not possibly begin their narrative at an earlier period in the life of Christ; and the oldest written Gospels, which were mere reproductions and collections of their oral teaching, of course covered the same space of time. From γενόμενοι it has been wrongly inferred that in the author's time those eye-witnesses already belonged to a past age, whilst in reality the past tense refers only to their quality as eye-witnesses and as first teachers.

In verse 3, which contains the apodosis, there is still another word liable to be misunderstood, παρηκολου-θηκότι. Jerome renders this clause by "assecuto omnia diligenter," but Eusebius (iii. 24. 15, and more clearly iii. 4. 6) understands the verb in the sense of "having followed," and consequently takes πᾶσιν as a masculine, referring it to the αὐτόπται καὶ ὑπηρέται. Like-wise Epiphanius (Against Heresies, 51, 7; ii. 458 ff.), in a free quotation, makes Luke say, παρηκολουθηκότι τοῖς αὐτόπταις . . . γενομένοις. Now, although it is quite possible that Luke had at some time seen one or more of the Twelve, it would be a gross exaggera-tion if he asserted of himself that he had been from the beginning (ἄνωθεν) a constant follower of all the apostles; and besides it does not make very good

B

Greek to combine this παρακολουθεῖν with ἀκριβῶς. But Polybius and other Hellenistic authors employ the verb in the sense of studying, and there can be no doubt that Luke's use is the same. Ἄνωθεν means much the same as ἀπ᾽ ἀρχῆς; but here it seems to imply something more than ἀπ᾽ ἀρχῆς in the preceding verse, since the relation between this ἄνωθεν and the following narrative, which starts at the earliest possible point, cannot well be denied. Καθεξῆς, belonging to γράψαι, might seem to contain a criticism on Luke's predecessors; but I do not think there is any trace of criticism in the whole proem. We know from a passage of Papias (Euseb. *Hist. Eccl.* iii. 39. 15), that Mark's Gospel had been criticised from very ancient times as not giving the events in their historical order; but Luke could not possibly introduce a better order, nor is there anything like orderly chronological narrative in the middle and largest part of his own Gospel; so it would be absurd if he promised to do what he neither could do nor has done. But Papias does not employ the adverb καθεξῆς: he says οὐ μέντοι τάξει, and καθεξῆς seems to me to have quite a different meaning, referring to the *uninterrupted* series of a complex narrative. Thus, in Acts xi. 4, we are told that Peter ἐξετίθετο αὐτοῖς (to his fellow-apostles) καθεξῆς, or, according to the western text, πάντα καθεξῆς (as we have in the proem πᾶσιν side by side with καθεξῆς), that is "completely," not breaking the series by any omission. The series was, in Peter's case, given by the historical order of events; but it might be given also by a mere manner of narration, and it cannot be Luke's meaning that Peter did not invert the order of facts, but only that he did not omit any important fact. On κράτιστε it will suffice to say that this epithet was the ordinary one in epistolary and oratorical style, when the person addressed was in a somewhat exalted position. So, in the Acts, Paul says, κράτιστε Φῆλιξ, κράτιστε Φῆστε (xxiv. 3; xxvi. 25), and in the dedication of books κράτιστε occurs when the person addressed is something like a patron, whilst φίλτατε denotes familiarity.[1] Who Theophilus was nobody knows, nor is there any reliance to be placed upon the tradition that he was the first bishop of Antioch, although, as Luke himself was a native of that town, we may conjecture, as ancient writers might, that he addresses a fellow-citizen. At any rate we may safely suppose that Theophilus did not live in Judaea, and that he was, like the author, of Greek extraction. He had been previously instructed in Christianity, but not by any authoritative person, so that he must desire a fuller and more trustworthy knowledge than he had hitherto

---

[1] *See* Otto in his edition of the *Epistle to Diognetus*, p. 79 ff. (p. 53 ff.).

received. For κατηχήθης does not denote more than "you have been informed," not characterizing the information as trustworthy; so, in Acts xxi. 21, κατηχήθησαν is directly used of wrong information. We have to acknowledge therefore a certain opposition between κατηχήθης and ἀσφάλειαν, and again between this verb and παρέδοσαν in verse 2 : παραδιδόναι is always used of communicating one's own knowledge to others as it is, without alteration. The Christian community of Judaea, the ἡμεῖς of verses 1, 2, already possessed that full and unadulterated knowledge, because they had been taught by the eye-witnesses themselves; but Theophilus lived outside the circle which the apostles had up to that time served with their preaching. Now he is to obtain, by means of Luke's Gospel, the same certainty on all particulars which was enjoyed by the inhabitants of Judaea; the time had come when oral teaching was to be supplanted by written teaching, and the perishable impression produced upon a few hearers by the preaching of the apostles was converted, by means of letters, into an imperishable and widely diffused treasure for mankind.

CHAPTER III.

WHEN DID ST. LUKE WRITE?

IT is a most natural question at this point: When did the change described at the close of the last chapter take place? It is easy to answer: some time before Luke wrote; for the proem itself manifestly declares that Gospel-writing had begun in Judaea, and was extended by Luke beyond that limit. But then it will be asked again: When did Luke write? I answer: As soon as he could; for there was no reason whatever for postponing a work, the usefulness of which was self-evident, and which must be required in any Greek or Roman town, where the preachers of the gospel went and found some willing hearers. People would ask the preachers: Who was that Jesus? What was His teaching? How did it come to pass that He was so cruelly murdered by His countrymen? and a countless number of similar questions, which could not be answered so easily by everybody as they may be nowadays.

Let us try to represent to ourselves the reality of things, as it must have been. Paul and Barnabas went together, for instance, to Antioch in Pisidia, and began to preach there to both Jews and Gentiles. They had been orally instructed by the eye-witnesses, and were now instructing others in the same way, successfully, as we see. The adherents they gathered were eager to spread the gospel to others, and so it rapidly went throughout the whole district (Acts xiii. 49). Of course Paul and Barnabas knew much fewer of the particulars than Peter did, and again their disciples knew less than Paul and Barnabas, and so the store of knowledge went on diminishing by expansion. That this was a very imperfect state of things, even from the first, is self-evident, and in progress of time it must have become more and more intolerable, even if we assume that writing, as an aid for memory, was in some measure employed. But, at any rate, those writings were very scanty, and very far from meeting the necessities which must arise at every moment. There were, in Antioch or Iconium, or in any of those towns where Christian communities had been founded, plenty of books of every kind. We see from the excavations recently made in Oxyrhynchos in Egypt what a number of books existed in a small provincial town, the fragments of which are now coming to light. Among the books in Antioch were the sacred books of the Jews, and any Christian might read as often as he would the predictions of the prophets about that Jesus, whom he believed to be his only Saviour. But on the fulfilment of those predictions, on the life of his Saviour, on His teaching, on His death and resurrection, not one of the many books of his town gave him a syllable of information. Was not this quite intolerable? The neighbour or friend of that Christian was anxious to learn something about the Jewish man whom he adored; what could he answer to the manifold questions of his friend? "Go to our preachers, or elders, or prophets; they will teach you more than I can." The man went there, and they taught him something more; but how much can that have been? In the natural and ordinary course of things, it may seem impossible that a religious sect so scantily provided with means of instruction, and so widely separated from its original birthplace, would maintain itself, or even increase, for any length of time; and if we must assume that this particular case was not an ordinary one, but quite exceptional, the necessity, nevertheless, of fuller instruction would be eagerly felt, and there would be in every town many more than

one Theophilus, who wanted to know "the certainty
of those things in which they had been instructed."
So I again say, Luke wrote as soon as he could.
When could he write? When he had provided
himself with full information. When was that time?
After the first Gospels had been written, and after
Luke had come into contact with that remnant of
primitive Christianity which existed in Judaea after
the departure of the apostles: in other words,
after he had himself become one of the "we,"
among whom the original teaching of the apostles
was preserved. These are two means of determining
the time; let us try to make as much as we can
out of each of them.

We have seen, in the preceding chapter, that
Gospel-writing was in the beginning a restoring, from
memory, of what the apostles had told in their
sermons, and what now could no longer be heard from
them, because they had finally left their native
country. As soon as that departure had taken place,
the necessity of restoring and preserving their teaching would be felt, and within one year, or two years
at most, that necessity might be provided for. So all
depends on fixing the time of that final departure.
We read in the Acts (i. 8) that the apostles had
received commission from their Lord to preach the
Gospel in Jerusalem, and in Judaea, and in Samaria,

and in every country of the earth. They acted accordingly, beginning in Jerusalem, and after some time
proceeding into Judaea and Samaria (Acts viii.-x.);
as regards the rest of their doings Luke leaves us
without information, and from Paul we learn only
this, that Peter went as far as Antioch in Syria (Gal.
ii. 11). But indirectly the Acts inform us that at the
time of Paul's last visit to Jerusalem (Acts xxi.)
all the apostles had departed, because they are not
even mentioned in the narrative. "The next day,"
says Luke (xxi. 18), "Paul went in with us unto
James, and all the *elders* were there." Compare the
words in xv. 4, about Paul's former visit: "And when
they were come to Jerusalem, they were received of
the Church, and of the *apostles and elders*." There is,
moreover, an ancient tradition preserved by Clemens
and by Eusebius, that Jesus had instructed His disciples to stay in Jerusalem twelve years, and after
that time to go out into the world.[1] Now, it is well
known that the chronology of our Lord's life and of
His disciples' lives is very far from being satisfactorily

---

[1] Clem. *Al. Strom.* vi. 5. 43 : διὰ τοῦτό φησιν ὁ Πέτρος (an apocryphal writing bearing the name of Peter) εἰρηκέναι τὸν κύριον τοῖς
ἀποστόλοις· . . . μετὰ δώδεκα ἔτη ἐξέλθετε εἰς τὸν κόσμον, μή τις (of the
Jews) εἴπῃ· οὐκ ἠκούσαμεν. Euseb. *Hist. Eccl.* v. 18. 14, speaking
of Apollonius (a writer in Phrygia against Montanism) says : ἔτι δὲ
ἐκ παραδόσεως τὸν σωτῆρά φησι προστεταχέναι τοῖς αὐτοῦ ἀποστόλοις ἐπὶ
δώδεκα ἔτεσι μὴ χωρισθῆναι τῆς Ἱερουσαλήμ.

established, and I do not purpose to solve, or even to discuss, these intricate questions in the present little book. But, at any rate, the doubts do not extend to more than four or five years, more or less; and if I simply adopt, upon the whole, the chronology of the ancients, the error, if there is any, cannot be said to be important. The *Chronicon Paschale* places the former of the two visits of Paul, of which we are speaking, under the consulship of Asiaticus and Silanus, that is to say, in the year 46 A.D.; for the later visit we have Eusebius' computation, according to which it falls in 54 A.D. The twelve years mentioned in the tradition do not agree with those dates, but the difference will not be very great if we place the departure of Peter and his fellow-apostles in 47 or 48. For the visit of Peter to Antioch, mentioned by Paul apparently in connection with his own visit to Jerusalem (Gal. ii.), seems to me to be nothing less than the first stage in a long journey, which conducted him finally to Babylon. Everybody knows that passage in the Epistle to the Galatians, where Paul relates that he and the apostles at Jerusalem parted amicably, under the agreement that he himself should go to the Gentiles, and Peter and the others to the Jews. Everybody knows the absurd interpretation given by some modern theologians, who add to the positive clauses of the agreement the corresponding negative ones: accord-

ing to these expositors, Peter was under obligation not
to convert any Gentile, and likewise Paul not to convert any Jew. As the Acts contain numerous instances
of Paul's trying to convert Jews, in every place where
he went, they conclude that the narrative of the Acts
is utterly untrustworthy. Paul went to Corinth, and
found there a Jew, say Aquila, who showed some
inclination to adopt the religion of Christ, but first
wanted better information. Now, if we believe the
theologians in question, Paul was obliged to say to the
Jew: "I have no right to convert you; you must go
to Peter." "Where is Peter?" "I don't know, very
likely in Babylon." But, putting aside these absurdi-
ties, we must try to understand the real meaning of
this agreement. As it was evidently impossible to
draw a line of separation between the Jews and Gentiles of one town, or of one district, and as Peter was
not to remain in Judaea, but obliged to go "to the end
of the world," there is but one partition possible : Paul
had to go to the West, where the Gentiles or, to speak
more correctly, the Greek Gentiles formed the
majority and the Jews the minority, and Peter to the
East where there was a small minority of Greeks, and a
very large number of Jews mixed up with Gentiles who
spoke the same language with the Jews, viz., Aramaic.
There Peter was in his proper place, as Paul would not
have been; conversely, in Corinth or Ephesus or Rome,

Paul was in his proper place, and Peter not. Now, Babylon appears as the town from which Peter sent out his (first) epistle, and Antioch lay on the route from Jerusalem to Babylon. " But "—I shall answer only one " But," and must refrain from entering into the interminable field of controversy which surrounds Peter's epistle and Peter's person—" but the real Babylon was at that time a deserted town, as Strabo attests; therefore the Babylon of the epistle must be the apocalyptic Babylon, that is to say, Rome." I answer, that Strabo attests nothing of the kind, but only that, of the immense space contained within the ancient walls of Babylon, which extended for the length of about forty-five miles, far the larger part lay waste, and that therefore one might well apply to Babylon the line of a comic poet on Megalopolis in Arcadia : ἐρημία μεγάλη ᾽στὶν ἡ μεγάλη πόλις (Strabo, p. 738). But still the large town had a great many inhabitants, although the neighbouring Seleucia had more. We might as well say the same of modern Rome, when we stroll from the Capitolium to the Colosseum and beyond, or to Mount Palatinus, or to other parts which are enclosed by the ancient fortifications. As for the epistle, it is sent (*see* i. 1) first to Pontus, Galatia, Cappadocia, lastly to Asia Proper and Bithynia, which agrees admirably with Babylon as the starting-point; but, if that starting-point had been

Rome, we may say with certainty that Asia would come first in the address, and not remote Pontus.

But it is time to turn back to our own starting-point. Peter then went away from Jerusalem in or shortly after the year 46, and with him, or before him, or shortly after him, the rest of the Twelve; and the necessity of a written Gospel, containing and conserving the matter of Peter's past sermons, immediately arose in Jerusalem itself, where that necessity hitherto had least been felt. I say again: if anybody prefers the year 48 to 46, or the year 50, or even 51-2—as Theodor Zahn does in his recent introduction to the New Testament—, I have no mind to dispute that point at present, as it will not affect the relative chronology of events, which is more important to me than the absolute dates. If Paul's visit to Jerusalem and the meeting of the apostles and elders (Acts xv.) was in the winter of 46-7, Paul's visit to Corinth may have been in the spring of 49, and his first visit to Ephesus, from which he immediately left for the East, in the autumn of 50; if we follow Zahn, the dates are respectively 51-2, 52 (November,—December), 54 (Whitsuntide). Now, after Paul had left Ephesus, Apollos went there, a Jew born at Alexandria, who " had been instructed in the way of the Lord (in

his native town, as the Western text inserts), and
being fervent in the spirit, he spoke and taught
diligently the doings of the Lord, knowing only the
baptism of John" (Acts xviii. 24 f.). Here we
meet with a Christian, who was at the same time
uncommonly well informed about the doings of Jesus,
and utterly ignorant about the rite of Christian
baptism, which the apostles had practised from the
beginning. Evidently he had had a teacher of the
same kind, who had not even baptized him after
the Christian rite, but, on the other hand, had
instructed him in a great many particulars generally
unknown to Christians. You see at once that such
a person is little less than an impossibility. Any
person who had been in contact with the eye-
witnesses, and learned from them, could not but
have learned the Christian rite of baptizing, and
Apollos did not even know that rite. So there
seems to be here an enigma very hard to solve.
But what right have we to bring in the "person"?
Are there not impersonal teachers, viz., books?
Apollos had come into possession of a written
Gospel, and had been instructed by that, which
could neither baptize him, nor teach him anything
about that rite, if it did not mention it. Now,
this is not only possible, but is actually the case
in St. Mark, that is to say, in the genuine Mark,

which closes at xvi. 8. I do not infer that Apollos
had got Mark's Gospel, but only say, if Apollos
possessed a copy of a Gospel, either that of Mark
or of any other with a similar conclusion, the whole
difficulty is quite easily and satisfactorily explained.[1]
We find therefore in the year 50 (or, according to
Zahn, 54) a written Gospel not only in existence,
but already rather widely spread. Is this possible,
and is it consistent with our former statements?
Let us see, and let us not take the dates, but the

---

[1] It has been argued against this solution, that the word
κατηχημένος, used of Apollos (Acts xviii. 25), implies oral and not
written instruction. I do not think that κατηχούμενος ἐκ τοῦ νόμου
(Rom. ii. 18) is to be understood of a Jew who did not read in
the Law himself, but heard it read and explained by others ; and
the interpretation of "having been catechized in his youth," given
by Mr. A. Wright, in the Expository Times (Oct. 1897, p. 9 f.),
is in direct opposition with the present tense. But if κατηχεῖσθαι
must stand always for oral instruction, much more must ἀκούειν
do so. Now we find in Plato (Phaedr. 268 C) : ἐκ βιβλίου ποθὲν
ἀκούσας οἴεται ἰατρὸς γεγονέναι, "having been informed by some book
he thinks he has become a physician." Here again, Mr. Wright
seems to me to misinterpret the words, by making them imply
that the man in question could not even read a book himself,
that is, that he was more ignorant than the sausage-dealer of
Aristophanes (see Knights v. 189). But there are more passages
of the same kind, in Plato and in later writers (see the Thesaurus
Gr. linguae s.v. ἀκούειν) : for instance, Dionysius, Antiquit. Rom.
i. 48, has οἱ ἀκούοντες in the sense of "my readers." Well, you
will say, it was a general custom in antiquity to have a book read
to oneself by a slave or some other person. And is not Apollos
included in that same antiquity? Let κατηχεῖσθαι be employed of
hearing even in the passage of the Acts : the book will still be there.

events only. Peter, having finally left Jerusalem, went to Antioch, and found Paul and Barnabas still there. This seems to indicate that that visit of Peter happened shortly after Paul's visit to Jerusalem ; for it is not to be supposed that the latter long delayed the communication of the apostles' decree to the congregations of Cilicia and Lycaonia (Acts xv. 40 ff. ; xvi. 4). A short time after Peter's visit, Paul started on his own journey, which must have taken him some time, even while it was still confined to the different countries of Asia (Acts xv. 40—xvi. 8). Meantime, the Gospel in question might be written in Jerusalem. Paul went over to Macedonia ; a copy of the Gospel (for such copies would be made at once) was brought to Alexandria. Paul went to Corinth and made there a stay of one year and six months, during which time he converted a great many Corinthians ; that same time was more than sufficient for Apollos to study the Gospel and to be converted by its means. Paul went to Ephesus, and from there to Syria, and so on ; Apollos came to Ephesus. Why might not all this really happen ? There are, at least, no chronological objections to our suppositions. As for years and dates, I only add that those of Zahn, as given above, seem to me not to grant sufficient space for Paul's journey from Antioch to Corinth, and especially for the former part of it, from Antioch to Troas; whilst, if we make Paul start early in 47, and come to Corinth early in 49, we may assign about six months to the journey through Macedonia, and eighteen to that through Asia. But, as I said before, I do not lay much stress at present on these differences of chronology.

We have sought and apparently found an answer to the first of our problems, viz., when the first written Gospels came into existence, and must now try to find an answer to the second. When did Luke become one of the "we"? Here we meet with no difficulty. Luke testifies himself (making use of the first person of the plural) that he went with Paul to Jerusalem in the spring of 54 (according to the chronology of the ancients), and left Palestine, again as a companion of Paul, as late as 56 (about August). During this period of more than two years, he was a member of the Christian community in Judaea, and at the end of it he was fully competent to write to Theophilus, let us say to Antioch : " the things which have come to pass among *us*," the more so as he could not be aware for what length of time he was still to remain in Judaea. That these two years afforded very ample time for collecting and studying written Gospels and gathering oral information, and for writing a Gospel

C

of his own, it is almost unnecessary to state. So I think that Luke finished his Gospel in the year 56, if we follow Eusebius, or, if any one prefers Zahn's chronology, in the year 60.

CHAPTER IV.

ARGUMENTS FOR AND AGAINST THE EARLY DATE OF ST. LUKE'S GOSPEL.

I AM well aware, that this early dating of Luke's Gospel is in direct opposition to opinions most current at the present day, according to which not one of our Gospels was composed much earlier than the destruction of Jerusalem (71), and Luke's Gospel later than that event. Professor Harnack, in his most recent publication, even while stating that now the tide has turned, and that theology, after having strayed in the darkness and led others into darkness (*see* Matt. xv. 14) for about fifty years, has now got a better insight into things, and has come to a truer appreciation of the real trustworthiness of tradition, still puts Mark's Gospel between 65 and 70 A.D., Matthew's between 70 and 75, but Luke's much later, about 78-93. Has that confessedly untrustworthy guide of laymen, scientific theology, after so many errors committed during fifty years, now of a sudden become a trustworthy one? Or have we good reason to mistrust it, as much, or even more, than we had before? In ordinary life no sane person would follow a guide who confessed to having grossly misled him during the whole former part of a journey. Evidently that guide was either utterly ignorant of the way, or he had some views and aims of his own, of which the traveller was unaware, and he cannot be assumed now to have acquired a full knowledge, or to have laid those views and aims wholly aside. Nevertheless, let us examine what reasons there may be for a later dating of Luke's writings, after having first glanced at the second part of them, viz., at the Acts.

As the second part of a work is later than the first, an early date of the Acts implies an even earlier one for the Gospel, and we might have started from the Acts and arrived at the same conclusions for the Gospel, if we had not chosen to go the opposite way. For that the Acts were composed in Rome, during the two years of Paul's first captivity which the Acts attest (xxviii. 30), is an assumption made as early as Jerome, who says of that book (*de Viris Illustribus*, 7): *in urbe Roma compositus est, id quod intelligitur ex eo, quod non ultra quartum annum Neronis rerum gestarum memoriam Lucas vertexuit.*

The fourth year of Nero is the year 58 ; more correctly
we should take the year 59, since Paul, if he started
for Rome in 56, did not arrive there before 57, and
the two years of the captivity extend from 57 (spring)
to 59 (spring). But the argument of Jerome is quite
clear: Luke would have continued his narrative and
not left it abruptly at this point, if he had known
anything more at the time he wrote; so the actual
end of the narrative must coincide with the time of
finishing the book. The same argument is given more
explicitly by Euthalius, in his preface to Paul's
Epistles,[1] and the scholars who lived after the
Renaissance and the Reformation of the Church have
adhered to it, not imagining that there would come a
time when this candid way of reasoning would be
abandoned for artificial ones, of which our ancients
could have no idea. One of these artificial reasonings
is this: Luke had the intention of writing a third
treatise ($\tau\rho\acute{\iota}\tau o\varsigma$ $\lambda\acute{o}\gamma o\varsigma$), which was to contain the
narrative from the end of Paul's first captivity down
to his second and to his death, and therefore he ter-
minated his second part at the point where he actually
does, reserving the rest (which was of course, as
far as the main events were concerned, already known
to his readers) for the third part. I quite agree,
that under this supposition the facts find a sufficient

[1] *See* Zacagni, *Monum. vet.*, p. 531.

explanation; but the supposition itself seems to me
not only unnecessary, but totally unfounded. If I
make a supposition not warranted by any testimony
(as there is no shadow of a trace of such a third part),
I must have and give good reasons for it; otherwise
the supposition will be discarded as arbitrary. Now
there is one reason which may impose on those who
are not thoroughly acquainted with New Testament
grammar, namely this: Luke says in Acts i. 1, that
the Gospel has been his πρῶτος λόγος, and πρῶτος
implies more than two, like *primus* in Latin. So it
does in old Greek; but in New Testament Greek the
distinction between the comparative and the super-
lative, of which this is one instance, has been altogether
abandoned, and as μείζων stands for μέγιστος, where
three things are compared, so πρῶτος regularly occu-
pies the place of πρότερος, where there are but
two (like English " first " and " second"). It must
be said, moreover, that the close of the Acts,
even if there was nothing to follow, is by no means
abrupt, since Luke has followed the course of the
Gospel from Jerusalem to Rome, from the Jews to
the Gentiles, and might well end his work with its
successful preaching in the centre of the world. But,
on the other hand, if he had known at that time the
final release of Paul, of whose former trials he has
told us so minutely, he would not have omitted to

indicate that much desired result, even if he chose not to enter into details, which he reserved for another volume. You will say, why did he not await the result, before closing his book? Because (I should answer) in the case of a speedy release of Paul the Romans, for whom he partially wrote, would learn it as soon as himself, and the Christians in other parts of the world, especially Theophilus, could not remain ignorant of so important a fact, but must hear of it before Luke's book would reach them; so there was no necessity to await further events, the exact time of which was quite uncertain. Besides, we must always bear in mind that the course of the Gospel was for the author (as for any Christian) the primary thing, and the fortunes of persons the secondary thing, even those of the principal persons, not to speak of subordinate agents like himself, whose doings he does not stoop to tell at all. But as I said before, if he had possessed further knowledge of the events, he would not have withheld a few words about them, as the main person of his narrative was therein so eminently concerned. If therefore the Acts were finished in the year 59, it clearly follows that the Gospel must have been written at the time we have already stated.

And now for the theologians, who assert that Luke's Gospel must be later than the destruction of Jerusalem. The reason is, of course, that the catastrophe of the holy city is told in the Gospel; that is to say, that Luke makes Jesus foretell it, which is quite sufficient, for coarse and vulgar reasoning, to lead to the conclusion that the author wrote after the event. *Omne vaticinium post eventum.* My readers must not be afraid that I am going to enter into a theological discussion of this axiom, since philology and history are quite sufficient to deal with it, as far as is needed here. But theologians may perhaps cry out, that I am treating them unfairly, ascribing to them that coarse and vulgar reasoning which they will pathetically disclaim. And yet you will find in Professor Weiss's Introduction that St. Matthew's Gospel is to be put later than 71, because of the verse, xxii. 7: "But when the king heard thereof, he was wroth: and he sent forth his armies, and destroyed those murderers, and burned up their city." But Professor Harnack is not shocked by this prediction, nor by any other in Matthew or in Mark; so his argument cannot be that vulgar one: *Omne vaticinium post eventum.* Very well. I do not intend to treat anybody unfairly, and the question is not one of persons, except as they exemplify the general tendency of a school or of an age. Now, it is undeniable that the axiom: *Omne,* etc., underlies the work of that theological school, which has, as Harnack says, misled the world for fifty years, and so we must deal with it, and prove the antithesis: *Non omne vaticinium post eventum*, which will be proved, if I adduce one certain instance of a vaticinium *ante eventum*. I might go to the Old Testament, and take Micah's prophecy of the destruction of Jerusalem, which is quoted in Jeremy; but as I need give only one instance, I prefer modern history to the Old Testament, and Jerome Savonarola to Micah. That prophet—for such he claimed to be—was burnt in 1497; his sermons were printed partly in his lifetime, partly shortly after his death, and prove that there have been and may be prophecies not only spoken or even written before the event, but actually printed before it. Accidentally, you will say, the event corresponded to the prophecy. But that is not my point, whether it was accidental, or the prophet had really foreseen the event; for in the case of the prophecies recorded by Luke you may raise the same controversy if you like. Most probably you will not like to do so, but will try to substitute the author for the prophet in order to get rid of the prophecy. But whether of Luke or of Christ, the prophecies are these: Luke xix. 43 f.: "For the days shall come upon thee, that thine enemies shall cast a trench about thee, and compass thee round," and so on (which prophecy is found in Luke alone); and xxi. 20 ff.: "And when ye shall see Jerusalem

compassed with armies, then know that the desolation
thereof is nigh," and so on (which prophecy is related in a somewhat different form by Matthew and
Mark). I do not think that either the former or
the latter of these foretellings is very distinct, since
there are neither names given, nor peculiar circumstances indicated; only the common order of events
is described: before the destruction the capture,
before the capture the siege and the circumvallation;
together with the destruction, the killing of the
inhabitants, and the leading away of others into
captivity, and then the Gentiles' taking possession
of the vacant soil; in all these particulars there is
nothing but the idea of destruction of the holy city
prepared and developed. There is still another prophecy: that the temple would be utterly destroyed,
so that no stone should be left upon another; but
as this one is common to the three synoptic Gospels,
and our critics have absolved Matthew and Mark of
the crime of falsified foretellings, we shall leave it,
although it is indeed much more peculiar, out of the
present discussion. On the other hand, Savonarola
foretold, as early as 1496, the capture of Rome,
which happened in 1527, and those sermons of 1496
were printed in 1497. I must not weary my readers,[1]

[1] I have treated this subject more copiously in a paper printed
in *Neue Kirchliche Zeitschrift*, 1896, 964 ff. *See* Villari, *la Storia di
G. Sav.*, 2nd ed. in 2 vols., Florence, 1887-8.

else I might give many passages which agree astonishingly well with the account given by contem-
poraries of that memorable event, for Savonarola
entered into particulars, and such particulars as were
indeed very hard to foresee. Especially remarkable
is this, that he extends the devastation to the churches
of Rome, which, in any ordinary capture by a Catholic
army, would have been spared, but in this case were
not at all respected, because a great part of the con-
quering army consisted of German Lutherans, for
whom the Roman Catholic churches were rather
objects of hatred and contempt than of veneration.
Now Lutheranism did not exist in 1496. Among
Savonarola's prophecies we find this one: " Rome,
thy churches will be made stables for the horses,
which they will place therein." In striking accordance with this, Guicciardini, one of the eye-witnesses
of the capture, says in his narrative: " You might
see the sumptuous palaces of the cardinals, the sacred
churches of St. Peter and St. Paul, and the other holy
places, which were formerly full of plenary indulgences
and of venerable relics, now reduced to stables of
horses, and instead of hypocritical ceremonies and of
wanton music, you might hear in them the pawing
and neighing of horses."[1]   I think it quite unnecessary

[1] *See* C. Milanesi, *Il Sacco di Roma del* MDXXVII (Flor. 1867),
where the original documents, and among them the narrative of
Luigi Guicciardini, have been reproduced.

to dwell any more on this topic, the general possibility
of *vaticinia ante eventum* having now been fully
established.

But there have also been written *vaticinia post
eventum*, and many more than *ante eventum*. Of
course this is quite true, and on the score of general
probability the prophecies in Luke might seem more
likely to belong to the former class than to the
latter. My object, however, is not to prove a particular, but to disprove an universal proposition;
it would be foolish to enter into any proof that
Luke's prophecies were really written *ante eventum*.
But the objection itself, you will say, is wrongly
presented: Professor Harnack, for instance, might
put it in this form. " We have the same prophecy
in the earlier Gospels in a somewhat veiled and
obscure shape (which is true with the important
exception of the prophecy concerning the temple);
on the other hand, Luke gives it in an explicit
and developed form. The real words of Christ
were most probably like those in Matthew and
Mark, but after the event the words were shaped
differently in order to fit them to the event." By
Luke? That I deny, and very decidedly. Luke
has given what he found, without adulteration; we
can easily distinguish a compiler of given materials
from one who moulds them artificially, and we clearly

see in Luke everywhere the raw material, whilst Matthew, that is to say the composer of the Gospel bearing Matthew's name, is much more liable to the charge of artificial shaping. Then, you will say, the author whose writing Luke used, or if not that author himself, the oral tradition which was his source, brought the prophecies into this developed form, whilst Matthew and Mark must represent the original words of Christ. Why? Because Mark is certainly earlier than Luke. But if there was, as you supposed, another written source for Luke, besides Mark, how will you prove that that source too was later than Mark? Because the developed form is always later than the undeveloped one. And thus we are gliding into an interminable and hopeless discussion of general probabilities.

But I hope it will be granted on all sides, that Luke really had, for his 21st chapter and those which precede and follow it, a different source from Matthew and Mark. Now, according to Matthew (xxiv. 15) and Mark (xiii. 14), Christ says to His disciples: "When ye therefore shall see the abomination of desolation, spoken of by Daniel the prophet, stand in the holy place (whoso readeth, let him understand), then let them who be in Judaea flee to the mountains," and so on. The passage of Daniel referred to is this (ix. 26 f.): "And the people of the prince that shall

come shall destroy the city and the sanctuary; and
the end thereof shall be with a flood . . . and he
shall confirm the covenant with many for one week,
and in the midst of the week he shall cause the
sacrifice and the oblation to cease, and for the overspreading of abominations he shall make it desolate,
even until the consummation," etc. Surely this is
more explicit and developed than anything in Luke,
and the whole difference between him and the
others amounts to this, that they make Christ refer
His hearers to an Old Testament prophecy, whilst
Luke makes Him give Himself the contents of that
same prophecy. For instance, in Luke He says
(xxi. 24): Ἰερουσαλὴμ ἔσται πατουμένη ὑπὸ ἐθνῶν,
ἄχρι οὗ πληρωθῶσιν καιροὶ ἐθνῶν; and in Matthew and
Mark He refers them to a passage where the Greek
words are: καὶ ἕως τῆς συντελείας καιροῦ συντέλεια
δοθήσεται ἐπὶ τὴν ἐρήμωσιν. So the real difference is
not between undeveloped and developed, but between
veiled and open, which is quite another thing. We
may suppose that Christ really did speak in both ways,
first referring to Daniel's prophecy, and then declaring
it Himself; for it is self-evident, that the real speech
of Christ must have been much longer than we read
it now in any Gospel. Of these two parts, Matthew
and Mark give the first, leaving out the second, and
Luke gives the second, leaving out the first.

There remain these questions, why Luke should
have left out the first, and why the others the
second? Now, Luke writing for Theophilus and
other Greeks, who were not very well acquainted
with the Old Testament, had good reason for leaving out the text of Daniel; conversely, Matthew
and Mark being Jews and writing for Jews, had a
very good reason to leave out the declaration. That
declaration was extremely painful for them, and
would be so for their readers. We see from the
Acts, that the apostles and their disciples were daily
frequenting the temple, which had by no means
ceased to be a most holy place for them, and to
learn that that place and the whole city was to be
laid waste could not but pain them to the utmost.
Who would not fain cast a veil over things the
aspect of which gives pain? And if we suppose,
as in my opinion we really must do, that the
Gospels were destined from the beginning to be read
in the weekly assemblies of the congregations, as
we have testimony to their having been read as
early as Justin's time (see *Apolog.* i. 67), and that
they were intended to be a substitute for the former
sermons of the apostles, the contents of which they
reproduced, then it might also be for safety's sake,
and in order not to give unnecessary offence to the
Jews, that the open prophecy of the destruction of

the holy city was left out. Stephen had said openly that the temple would be destroyed, and he had become the first martyr.

There is still another objection commonly made to Luke, viz., that he puts a distance of time between the end of Jerusalem and that of the world, whilst in Matthew and Mark these two events appear to be closely connected. Matthew has (xxiv. 29): "*Immediately* after the tribulation of those days shall the sun be darkened," and so on, and Mark (xiii. 24), a little less explicitly : " But in those days, after that tribulation, the sun," etc. But in Luke (xxi. 24 f.), the transition from the one prophecy to the other is made in this way : " Jerusalem shall be trodden down of the Gentiles, until the times of the Gentiles be fulfilled. And there shall be signs in the sun," etc. Now, it is argued, that Matthew and Mark, writing before or shortly after the destruction of Jerusalem, still expected the end of the world to be quite near at hand ; but Luke, writing later, had lived to see some interval of time, and therefore took care not to connect closely the two catastrophes. I might answer, that this explanation of the difference is one out of many which are equally possible, the more as Matthew and Mark themselves do not agree here in the words, and it is therefore impossible to assert either that Christ really said "immediately,"

or that He said "in those days." But the most
important thing is, that Luke's insertion, "until
the times of the Gentiles be fulfilled," is nothing
more than an explanatory paraphrase of Daniel's
ἕως συντελείας καιροῦ, and the passage of Daniel is
referred to in the other two. So there is in reality
much more agreement than at first there seemed to
be. As for the rest, we are fully at liberty to
trust Luke's account more than that of the other
two, who may have been partially influenced by
their being Jews. The destruction of the temple
and of the holy city was, in a Jew's eyes, next to the
end of the world (*see* Matt. xxiv. 3 ; Luke xxi. 7 β) ;
and as they were to make a transition from the
one prophecy to the other, they made that transition
in conformance with their own ideas, but each of
them in a different way, so that we may suppose
their common source to have contained neither
"immediately" (a very common word in the two
first Gospels, much less so in Luke and John), nor
"in those days" (also very common in the three
first Gospels). But as for Luke, he can hardly be
said not to have partaken in the common belief of
the first age of Christians, that the return of our
Lord and the final judgment was near at hand, as
long as he says like the others, after the *second*
prophecy (xxi. 32): "Verily I say unto you, This

D

generation shall not pass away till all be fulfilled."
It is true that there are here in Luke various
readings, which deserve at least a serious consideration. The Latin codex *i* has "it shall not pass
away from this generation until" etc., which makes
no great change of sense; but the Latin *e* has
instead of "this generation," *caelum istud*, "this
heaven," and this reading leads directly on to the
form found in Marcion's Gospel: "Heaven and earth
shall not pass away, unless all be fulfilled. Earth
and heaven" (note the inverted order of words)
"shall pass away, but my words shall not pass
away." The heretic Marcion, indeed, does not
deserve implicit confidence; but the Latin witness *e*
is above the suspicion of heretical tendencies, and
I am much inclined to regard Marcion's form as
the true one in Luke, whilst the other might very
easily come in by the way of assimilation to the
other Gospels, which has, as we shall see more fully
hereafter, much affected Luke's text. The sense
then will be this: "You may be quite sure that the
signs of which I have told you will come before
the end of things, and that the end will not come
abruptly, without those foregoing signs; so I have
rightly instructed you to give heed to them, in
order that you may be well prepared for the final
catastrophe." The verses immediately preceding in

Luke (29-31) are common in substance to the three synoptic Gospels; but not quite so what comes before them. Luke alone has verse 28 : " And when these things begin to come to pass, then look up, and lift up your heads, for your redemption draweth nigh," which is very well illustrated by the subsequent parable (29 ff.), and stands in close relation with the verse in question (32). So for internal as well as for external reasons—since of two readings in Luke, one of which exactly agrees with another Gospel, whilst the other is a peculiar one, the former is always liable to suspicion of assimilation—I do prefer Marcion's reading of this verse and of the next one, where the inversion " Earth and heaven " after " Heaven and earth " (32) cannot easily be deemed accidental.

But if this is true, you will say, that argument of the theologians which I am combating will receive additional strength. Be it so, the strength will not even then be too great. Those epistles of Paul, which are nearly contemporary to Luke's Gospel, Colossians, Ephesians, Philippians, Timothy, and Titus, while they are as full of references to the day of the Lord as those preceding in time, do not contain like them any clear expression of Paul's hope to live to see that day. He seems to have abandoned · that hope which he formerly cherished and why might not Luke be of the same mind, the more so if he did not find in the authors, whom he follows in his Gospel, any distinct warrant for these exaggerated hopes ? I do not think, indeed, that Mark and Matthew deserve such exclusive confidence in comparison with Luke, as many theologians are inclined to give them. Just because Luke is the later writer—compared with Mark,—he may well be the more correct one. And here we may abandon this subject, and pass to considerations of a different order.

CHAPTER V.

IMPORTANCE AND METHOD OF TEXTUAL CRITICISM IN THE NEW TESTAMENT.

No work of early literature which has been spared by time and has survived to this day—with a few exceptions not worth being mentioned here,—subsists in the original writing of the author, but in the writing of others, derived through a long series of successive copies from that original writing. Moreover, we do not ordinarily read it even in those written copies, but in a printed book which has been made from the copies, either directly or more often indirectly, being the last in another long series of successive printed editions. Nevertheless, we are used to regard that printed book, say a book printed in 1897, as substantially identical with the writing of the author. Generally we may safely do so, for that identity exists in the whole of the book and in most of its particulars; but if we come to care for any definite particulars, and are to draw inferences from them, the apparent identity may be, in a special case, a gross deception, and the inferences will be utterly wrong. Many and many a time, in cases concerning the Old or the New Testament, as well as in other cases, that deception has been practised upon readers by their book, and they have been misled by it into drawing wrong conclusions and adopting wrong opinions. We may indeed partly provide against such deceptions, either by consulting editions which come earlier in the series, or by going back to the written manuscripts, and as far back in the series of those manuscripts as we can. But to speak in exact terms, no two different editions are absolutely identical, nor are any two written copies, nor is any edition or copy identical with the original writing.

I was speaking just now of a well-known passage in Luke: "Verily I say unto you, this generation shall not pass away before all be fulfilled," that is to say, before the final catastrophe of the world come to pass. We know that in fact the generation of which the Lord is speaking has passed away to the last man, and many generations more, and still the final catastrophe has not come. So it appears as if our Lord had given us a false prediction. In order to avoid this conclusion which must seriously shock us, we may have recourse to various alternatives. We may, on the one hand, suspect that we have given a wrong interpretation to the words (which have been preserved in Greek). But upon consideration, this way will appear hardly practicable in this case, although it may be so in others, the instances of individual or even traditional misunderstandings of a passage being very numerous. Or we may question the accuracy of the account given by the Gospel-writer. This way seems to be open in every case; but the more we get used to it, the more we shall lose that confidence in the sacred writers, which is so important for our Christian faith. There is still one way more; that of suspecting the accuracy of the textual tradition, which has intervened between the author and ourselves. This way proved to be practical in this case of Luke's passage, at least for me, and I (or we) have by its means quite got rid of the difficulty, as far as it regards Luke; for Matthew and Mark are still there, attesting the false prediction. But the whole case has now become somewhat different; for the prophecy is now no more universally attested, and we may correct the one extant tradition by means of the other. It must be noted, however, that in this very case even the theologian does not have easy access to the sources of information. In ordinary editions of the New Testament, he will find nothing at all, and even in Tischendorf's large edition he will find only the reading of Marcion, but not its partial confirmation by the Latin codex *e*. He must needs consult the separate edition of that codex made by the same Tischendorf, that is to say, he must consult editions of all the different Greek or Latin or Syriac manuscripts, and seek for a different reading, and be lucky if at last he finds it. But how few can do this?

We pass to another consideration which leads in the same direction. The life of our Lord has of course been the object of so-called scientific investigation, although, in reality, there are only some particulars of it which come within the range of such investigation, while the real import of it lies far beyond. But now I am speaking just of these particulars, one of which is, that our Lord, after He was taken, was conducted either directly to the palace of Caiaphas the high priest (so the synoptic Gospels), or first to Annas the father-in-law of the high priest, (so the Gospel of John). The latter testimony seems to be more accurate and trustworthy; but then, the accuracy of the other narrative is rather seriously affected, not because it omits an intermediate station on the way, but because it refers the very important transaction, the trial of our Lord and Peter's denial, to a wrong locality; for John, as it seems, makes all this take place in the house of Annas. I say, "as it seems," for there is in reality no contradiction whatever between the Gospels, but only a slight and quite justifiable omission on the part of the three. Our John is not identical with the real John, and it will be quite clear even from a careful examination of the text as it stands, that John can neither have meant nor have written the commonly accepted account with Annas' house as the scene of the trial. "They led Him away to Annas first, for he was father-in-law to Caiaphas, which was the high priest that same year. Now Caiaphas was he, which gave counsel to the Jews, that it was expedient that one man should die for the people (see xi. 49 ff.). And Simon Peter followed Jesus, and so did another disciple : that disciple was known unto the high priest, and went in with Jesus into the palace of the high priest" (John xviii. 13 ff.). After having been distinctly told that Caiaphas was the high priest that year, and not Annas, we read that the other disciple went in with Jesus into the palace of the high priest. Whose palace, therefore ?   Of course that of Caiaphas. How has Jesus come there ? The writer, leaving that serious omission unexplained and uncorrected, goes on to speak not of Annas but of the high priest, and to tell of Peter's being introduced into his palace

(ver. 18), and then of Peter's first denial, and next not
of the second one, but of the trial of Christ. After
that, he suddenly says (ver. 24): "Now Annas sent
Him bound to Caiaphas the high priest." Then he
returns to Peter, telling of his second and third denials, and from Peter again to Christ (ver. 28):
"Then led they Jesus from Caiaphas into the hall of
judgment" (to Pilate). This narrative is so utterly
confused, that it is no wonder King James' trans-
lators tried to correct it by interpretation, giving in
ver. 24 not "sent" but, "had sent." But the Greek
words give no warrant for this interpretation, and
even if it were possible, we could not withhold our
censure of the writer, as he would then have told a
simple story in the most awkward way. In reality,
the blame is to be cast upon the textual tradition and
not upon the author, and we may learn from this
quite evident case, that those written copies (not to
speak of editions), which we are accustomed to rely
upon, by no means deserve implicit trust. Which
copies, then, do deserve it? No single copy at all,
but if anything the tradition taken as a whole,
with entire liberty to select in each individual case
that branch of the tradition for our guide which shall
seem to us to be in this case most trustworthy, even
if it is a heretical witness like Marcion. I deliber-
ately say, "if anything," for there may be cases in

which no branch of the extant tradition has preserved the true reading. In this very case of John's ch. xviii. until a few years ago there was no witness for it in its totality, although there were a very few for a part of the truth. But since Mrs. Agnes Smith-Lewis discovered and published the Syriac manuscript of Mount Sinai, we read in this one witness the following account: " They led Him away to Annas first, the father-in-law to Caiaphas, who was the high priest that same year (13). Now, Annas sent Him bound to Caiaphas (24); Caiaphas was he who gave counsel," etc. (14). Then comes the mention of Simon Peter and of the other disciple, and the statement that the latter went in with Jesus into the palace (15). Next comes (19-23) the story of the trial, and after that (16 ff.), " But Peter stood at the door without," and then the whole story of the three denials coherently, of course without the repetition standing in our texts: (18) " And Peter stood with them, and warmed himself," and (25): " and Peter stood and warmed himself." This is the narrative of a real author; the other one is that of blundering scribes.[1]

[1] I may note that Prof. F. Spitta (*Zur Geschichte und Litteratur des Urchristenthums*, 1893, pp. 158 ff.) got at a part of the truth in a purely conjectural way. He combines the two separated parts of the story of Peter's denial, and establishes this order: vers. 12, 13, 19-23, 24, 14, 15-18, 25b-28.

We shall speak later on of the condition in which John's Gospel has come down to us; for such gross misplacements are far from being a general feature in New Testament tradition. What I am now insisting upon is the absolute necessity of textual criticism for all studies connected with the New Testament. It is not a certain amount of textual criticism, which is required, but thorough and sound textual criticism, as even with that we shall often remain very far from the goal we want to attain.

Now it is a well-known fact that the number of various readings collected from the manuscripts of the New Testament by successive generations of scholars is already, and has long been, astonishingly great.[1] Nevertheless many men in Germany, and in England and elsewhere, are still engaged with praiseworthy zeal in increasing the number from fresh sources. Nor can it be said that this zeal is altogether misplaced, although it may be so in some cases. For I do not think that every manuscript ought to be thoroughly examined, because a great many of them very soon show themselves to be quite worthless, and it is even more strongly my opinion that not every collation of manuscripts ought to be put into print. On the other hand, we saw just now that there may still be hidden in some corner of Europe, or Asia, or Africa,

[1] There are estimated now to be about 150,000.

a veritable treasure of a manuscript, as that Sinai manuscript was until recent years. Nor will those treasures always present themselves in a very ancient and musty shape. There is in London a Greek manuscript of the Gospels, written in the eleventh century—that is to say comparatively very late—which was bought at some auction in the year 1882; it was examined by Dean Burgon first, then by W. H. Simcox, who published his collation in a journal, and lastly by H. C. Hoskier, who published his in a special book; and the pains they took have been requited by 270 new readings, hitherto found in no manuscript. In the passage of John's Gospel, of which we treated above, one Greek manuscript, dating from the end of the twelfth century, has preserved a part of the true reading. We must therefore not look simply to age, but to intrinsic value, which is to some extent independent of age. For it is quite possible that an ancient and valuable manuscript was carefully copied, say in 1500, and afterwards perished; the recent copy in this case will possess by inheritance all the merits of the lost archetype, side by side with which it would of course be worthless.

This therefore is the first task, to collect all the attainable materials for the restitution of the primitive text. A second will be to sift the materials, for by far the largest part of them is utterly worthless.

What, for instance, is the value of knowing, that in a given passage a given manuscript has εἶπε and not εἶπεν? or that Φαρισαῖοι is spelt therein with ει instead of ι? For a philologist this may have some value, in case the manuscript is very ancient; the spelling will teach him, that the ι in this word is long. But the *apparatus criticus* even of the largest edition ought to be disencumbered of such minutiae, which may be treated in a general way in the Prolegomena; for the editor himself must know more than he gives his readers. Moreover, as is nowadays the practice in editions of Greek and Roman profane writers, there must be a sifting of the manuscripts, and all those which have nothing good of their own must be discarded. Those endless lists of witnesses are not only very cumbersome, but quite worthless, since the decision on the correctness of a reading never depends on numbers. In this way, we shall get a comparatively short apparatus for most parts of the New Testament, although there are some books where no sifting will appreciably diminish the heap.

The condition, indeed, of the different writings combined into the New Testament is far from being equally good, or equally bad. There is, in the first place, a wide difference between them as regards the number of extant witnesses, which is exceedingly large for the Gospels, but much smaller for the other parts, the Acts and Catholic Epistles (which are usually contained in the same manuscripts), the Pauline Epistles, the Apocalypse (for which the number is smallest of all). Then the discrepancies between the manuscripts are comparatively small in number and importance in the case of all the epistles, which appear to have been handed down in as good and trustworthy form as any classical author. Here therefore the third task of a critic, that of discriminating and deciding between the various readings, is no more difficult than in the case of classical authors. I do not say that it is easy, either for these parts of the New Testament or for the classics; the term easy may apply to a great deal of patristic literature, which has come down to us nearly as it was written by the authors. But for the other writings contained in the New Testament, viz., the Gospels, Acts, and Apocalypse, the difficulties are much greater than they are, as a rule, in the classics, and more especially in some of the Gospels, where they reach an amount which perhaps is nowhere attained in any other literature. It is not only the great number of witnesses which makes the difficulty, for that number is equally great for Matthew and Luke, and nevertheless textual criticism in Matthew is comparatively easy, at least to one who has been occupied with the text

of Luke; but it is chiefly the wide divergencies between the witnesses which make one sometimes feel
burdened by a weight too great to be borne.

There is, indeed, a way to get rid of most of
those difficulties, that of discarding beforehand the
majority of the witnesses, not on the ground that
they are not independent (in which case the discarding is quite justified), but as untrustworthy. A
brief survey of the witnesses shows that, besides those
giving the common text as it was current in Byzantine
times, there are two main classes : one " Alexandrian,"
represented by the oldest uncials, Vaticanus B,
Sinaiticus ℵ and Alexandrinus A, and by other
MSS. besides; and one " Western," represented by the
old Latin versions and the Graeco-Latin Canta-
.brigiensis D, etc., in very close agreement with
the old Syriac versions. Now, if we had to deal
only with the former class our task would be
extremely simplified; because, although ℵ and B and
A are far from giving an identical text, their
divergencies are small in comparison with those
given by the Western witnesses. The editors of
the New Testament in our century, from Lachmann
to Westcott and Hort, have indeed thought themselves justified in relying chiefly upon Alexandrian
authority, and in neglecting more or less the Western
testimonies. The result would have been generally

speaking worse if they had chosen the opposite way, basing their text chiefly on Western authority and neglecting Alexandrian. There is among the former nothing to be compared with the latter for carefulness and for beauty of writing, for instance, with the Vaticanus B, which is thought to have been written as early as the fourth century, that is to say, two centuries earlier than the Cantabrigiensis D. So if a general option must be made between the two classes, nobody will hesitate to give his suffrage to B and to the Alexandrians. But such necessity is far from being the case: we are only bound to individual option in individual cases, and if that option may be justly influenced by a general preference given to the one class, we must always take heed not to let that influence prevail over the individual considerations. In order to see how unjust it would be wholly to neglect Western authority, let us take the example of the Epistle to the Romans. There is no doubt that the Roman Christians always held in great honour that precious treasure, which belonged in one sense to themselves exclusively: and yet are we for that same epistle wholly to disregard the testimony of Roman or Western witnesses, and to rely only upon Alexandria, where the original of that epistle certainly never came? Moreover, let us compare the position of a judge

E

who has to decide an intricate and very complex case, where there are many witnesses frequently contradicting each other. For many of the particulars, let it be quite evident that some of the witnesses have told a lie, and the others the truth; but in some few particulars let it be equally evident that the truth is on the side of the former witnesses, and the lie on that of the latter. Now, would it not be quite absurd for the judge, as regards the great bulk of particulars that might still be in dispute, simply to adhere to the statements given by those witnesses who have been convicted only of a few lies, and wholly to shut his eyes to all other evidence? On the contrary, he would say: All these witnesses are liars, nor does it matter how often a witness has been convicted of a lie, since everyone of them has been convicted of not always telling the truth; so I must rely on the evidence given by the facts themselves, and, not on the witnesses. But, if the critic acts on these principles, how will he be able to decide in everyone of the innumerable cases put before him? Is there always an evidence given by the facts themselves? Certainly not, and in these cases he will necessarily recur to the evidence of those witnesses who seem to him to be least untrustworthy, taking care, however, not to admit such cases more than is necessary. If his general appreciation of the witnesses is right, he may nevertheless decide wrongly in some cases, but rightly in the majority of them, and he will have fulfilled his task as well as is possible. It is an ideal task for a critic, a task lying far above his reach in the clouds, to restore the original form of the writing throughout; as things are, he will deserve commendation, if he has approached that form even by a small degree nearer than his predecessors.

There is still one more important question: Whether conjectural emendation is justified for the New Testament as well as for classical authors. Now, there can hardly be any critic who will absolutely deny that in a given case all manuscripts and versions may present a wrong reading, or wrong readings, and that the true one, lying not far behind the corruption, may be found by conjecture. But as the witnesses are for this book so very numerous, so early, and so independent of each other, such cases will be quite exceptional. Even if a right conjecture be made by a critic, the probability is, that on closer examination of the vast amount of existing external evidence, that true reading will be detected among that mass of testimonies, and the emendation will prove to be an attested variant.

I may give a few instances from the Acts. In xvi. 12 Philippi is described as being either πρώτη

μερίδος τῆς Μακεδονίας πόλις (Vatic. B), or πρώτη
τῆς μερ. Μακ. πόλις (Sin. ℵ etc.), or πρώτη τῆς
μερ. τῆς Μακ. πόλις (majority of manuscripts). D
in this case gives an evident gloss: κεφαλὴ τῆς
Μακεδ. πόλις, which is not even good Greek, but
coined after the Latin *caput Macedoniae.* The true
reading, viz., πρώτης μερίδος τῆς Μακ. πόλις (to
which B comes nearest of all, omitting but one σ),
was found by conjecture long ago by Pearce and
Clericus, who remembered that the Romans, after the
conquest of Macedonia, had divided the country, as
Livy (45. 29) relates, into four districts, of which
the eastern part with Philippi and Amphipolis was
number one, the latter city not the former being
the capital of that district. I admitted πρώτης into
my first edition of the Acts as a conjecture (which I
too had made independently); in my second edition,
which appeared a year later, it stands as an attested
reading. Whence did that attestation come? I
found it first of all in a Provençal mediaeval version,
which gives *en la primeira part de Macedonia*; next
the Paris Professor, Samuel Berger, called my attention to a codex of the Latin Vulgate, with *in prima
parte Mac.*; lastly, Professor E. Nestle pointed out
that the oldest German versions also give that same
reading (*zu dem ersten teyl zu M.,* or *des ersten teyls
zu M.*). But what kind of authority is all this? A

very slender one, you will say; but when a corruption has spread widely, as in this case, you must go to the very remotest corner, if you wish to find the true reading preserved.

Another case which I shall propose is different, in as far that the conjecture has not really been made so far as I know; nevertheless, it might have been made by a reflecting critic. In Acts vi. 9 the opponents of Stephen are said to have been τινὲς τῶν ἐκ τῆς συναγωγῆς τῆς λεγομένης Λιβερτίνων καὶ Κυρηναίων καὶ Ἀλεξανδρέων καὶ τῶν ἀπὸ Κιλικίας καὶ Ἀσίας. Now, we are utterly ignorant of a synagogue in Jerusalem bearing the name of Λιβερτίνων, or the Freedmen, and there is this additional difficulty, that the words καὶ Κυρηναίων καὶ Ἀλεξανδρέων seem to form a part of the same appellation, although Cyrenians and Alexandrians belong to definite towns, and freedmen existed everywhere. I have tried in my commentary to disjoin those words from Λιβερτίνων, and to bring them into connection with καὶ τῶν ἀπὸ Κιλικίας καὶ Ἀσίας; but the right way lay quite in an opposite direction. Mr. F. C. Conybeare and Mr. J. Rendel Harris directed my attention, some time afterwards, to Armenian versions of the Acts and of the Syriac commentaries on that book, and in those sources I found the reading *Libyorum* instead of Λιβερτίνων, a reading given already by Tischendorf, but at the first disregarded by me. Now, I saw at once that something like Λιβύων would suit the context very well indeed, as the Greek towns lying westwards from Cyrene would come quite appropriately under that designation. But can Λιβερτίνων be a corruption of Λιβύων? Of course not, nor does Λιβύων seem to be the right appellation for those Jews, as the Libyans were nothing but barbarous tribes. But Λιβυστίνων will both suit the sense, designing them as inhabitants of Libya, and come very near to the corrupted Λιβερτίνων, · there being but two letters different. It is easy to establish that this form of the adjective from Λίβυς was a current one, from Catullus' (60. 1) *montibus Libystinis*, and from the geographical lexicon of Stephanus Byzantinus, and so on. This therefore is the true reading, and the synagogue in question bore the name of Λιβυστίνων καὶ Κυρηναίων καὶ Ἀλεξανδρέων ; that is to say, of the African Jews in the geographical order of their original dwelling-places. In this case the true reading has been preserved in the remote East, whilst in the former it was from the remote West that the help came.

Of course, the fact that πρώτη in one of these passages, and Λιβερτίνων in the other, is almost universally attested, is not to be understood as being the result of one great deliberate action, viz., of a revision of the text made at a definite time

by definite men, and then imposed upon the whole
Christian Church. If such a revision had taken
place in the ancient Church, like those revisions
which have been made for instance at different
times in the English Church, we should certainly
hear of that fact from some of the numerous
ecclesiastical writers whose works have come down
to us. How, then, is that universal agreement in
blunders to be explained? By the separate and
continuous agency of a common practice, which
consisted in collating copies with each other, and
when discrepancies were found, correcting the more
recent copy by the older one. The Jews, - by
following this practice, have attained very nearly
absolute identity in their copies of the Old Testament; and the Christians, although they remained
far behind that extreme degree of accuracy and
scrupulosity, became nevertheless more and more
careful, lest their own sacred books might be
adulterated by corrupt readings. In the East this
care is to be seen much earlier than in the West,
where culture rapidly declined with the downfall of
the Roman Empire; but as we are dealing with
an originally Greek book, the Greek East comes
much more into our present consideration. The
care taken in revising and collating was by no
means confined to the sacred books, but extended

to classical writings as well. There can hardly be
a more serious mistake than when Byzantine scribes
are made responsible for the corruptions in classical
texts. Of course they committed blunders, partly
through ignorance and partly by inadvertence; but
in most cases ˙those blunders were removed by
correction, and we see from the remnants of ante-
Byzantine copies, which are coming to light in ever-
increasing number, that there is in most cases a
rather small difference between a copy, say of Plato,
of the fifteenth century and another of the fifth.
On the other hand, in the first centuries of our era
(and in those before, which do not come here within
our view), the work of revising and correcting was
in a great measure left to the buyer and owner of
a book, who might, if he liked, procure himself
another copy, and correct his own by means of that.
It is therefore not at all astonishing, that in the case
of the New Testament, as in other cases, the very
earliest copies may have been the most carelessly
made. Of course there was always a difference in the
matter of care or negligence between different contemporary copies, and in a later age, when men had become more careful and when they saw the damage
already done, they recurred to those of the ancient
copies still extant, which seemed to them to be
the most careful and trustworthy, and used those

copies as their standard for the correction of the
recent copies. Very likely their action was upon
the whole quite justified and extremely meritorious;
but whilst a number of blunders were abolished in
that way, some few were at the same time per-
petuated and became universal. For at the time of
which we speak, that from Constantine onwards, the
intercourse between the distant parts of the Church,
which had of course always existed, increased in
no small degree, that being the time when the
Oecumenical Council became an institution, and the
dogmatic controversies, which were to be decided by
the letter of the inspired books, required careful and
universally acknowledged copies of those books.   So
we must suppose, that from that time on not many
fresh corruptions of the sacred text were allowed to
exist or to spread, and that the differences remaining
between the individual copies date from an earlier
time, and might be supported by the authority of
ancient manuscripts.   But it is now time to close
these general considerations, and to treat more especially of the textual condition of the Gospels.

CHAPTER VI.

TEXTUAL CONDITION OF THE GOSPELS.
MATTHEW—LUKE.

THE union of the four acknowledged Gospels into
one *Euangelium quadripertitum* was effected, at
least ideally and theoretically, in the second century,
before Irenaeus, who tries to give even dogmatic
grounds for that number. It does not follow that
Irenaeus read them actually in a single volume,
the size of papyrus volumes or rolls being usually
not so large as to include more than one Gospel,
and papyrus rolls still prevailed in that age over
parchment books. Of course there had been a time
when the single Gospels had their quite separate
existence, and when Luke's Gospel, that is, Luke's
first book to Theophilus, still maintained its connection
with the Acts, that is Luke's second book to the
same Theophilus. A very curious trace of this
connection, as existing at least in the West for a

certain length of time, has been recently discovered. The name of John has in Greek two spellings, one with one N and another with two. I do not doubt that the former is the right one, and that from the Hebrew *Joohanan* Ἰωάνης sprang up in the same way as from *Jonathan* Ἰωνάθης or Ἰωνάθας, by converting the *an* into an accusative termination, and replacing the N by an Σ for the nominative. As there was another N before the vowel, and not a P or an I or E, the termination in $H\Sigma$ must have seemed more regular than that in $A\Sigma$, just as we have Ἰωνάθης in Josephus. But in a later age there crept in much irregularity in the doubling of the liquid consonants; Ἰωάννης is parallel, for instance, to Λουκίλλιος for *Lucilius*. Now the Vaticanus B, than which there is no more trustworthy witness in all matters of spelling, nearly always gives Ἰωάνης, whilst the Cantabrigiensis D has both spellings, but more frequently that with double N. The order of the books contained in D is this : Matthew, John, Luke, Mark, Acts. In the first two, the spelling with double N has a very large predominance : twenty-four instances to two in Matthew, and seventeen to seven in John ; but in the third Gospel, that of Luke, the writer of a sudden adopts the opposite principle, writing Ἰωάνης twenty-seven times and Ἰωάννης but once. This of itself would perhaps not be very astonishing; but when he comes to Mark, he falls back to his first spelling, there being in Mark twenty-four instances of Ἰωάννης, and but two of Ἰωάνης. Last comes the second part of Luke, and again he changes and spells Ἰωάνης twenty-one times, Ἰωάννης but twice.[1] That this definite inconsistency, and at the same time consistency, cannot have been effected by mere chance is quite evident, and there is but one explanation for it. First, we must acknowledge in the writer of D a degree of care which hitherto seemed to be wholly alien from him, the number of his blunders, more especially in the spelling of the words, being exceedingly great; we must now refer at least the greater part of these blunders to the archetype from which the writer copied. Again, if the archetype of D contained the same books in like order, the same remark must apply to the writer of that archetype. But perhaps there was a different order in the archetype, with Luke's Gospel coming last of the four. This too is an order attested elsewhere, or to speak more accurately, there are different attested orders with Luke as the last of all.[2] But even in this case the transition from one spelling to another requires

---

[1] On this important discovery (made by E. Lippelt), *see* my edition of St. Luke's Gospel, p. vi ff.   Three of the number have been corrected by my friend Prof. J. Rendel Harris.

[2] *See* E. Nestle's Introduction to the New Testament, p. 83 f.

TEXTUAL CONDITION OF THE GOSPELS.   77

a better explanation than that of chance, and the
supposition must necessarily be made, that the
archetype (or one of the archetypes) of D united
in itself parts coming from different sources, one
part of which consisted of the two books of Luke
written by one scribe.   And from this we see that
there had been a time when there was a closer
connection between Luke's first and second parts,
than between Luke's Gospel and the other Gospels;
a fact, besides, which must be credible independently
of all actual traces or testimonies.

In the first stage of its existence, therefore, every
Gospel was separate from other Gospels, and it is
self-evident that during that stage it cannot have
remained quite unaltered and unadulterated.   That
very first age was also, as we have seen, that of
least care in transcribing, and there was besides
another reason for corruptions of a special kind.
Let us take the case of an individual Christian, or
of a single Christian community, possessing but one
copy of one Gospel.   Now he or it might come into
contact with another individual or community in
possession of a different Gospel.   Nothing would be
more natural than the wish to compare the two
Gospels, and to supplement, or even to correct, one
from the other.   Let Luke's Gospel be the one, and
Matthew's the other: the former bore the name

of a later disciple, whose master himself, viz., Paul, had not belonged to the eye-witnesses, and the other bore the name of an apostle, one of the eye-witnesses. Naturally Matthew must appear to be more trustworthy than Luke, and accordingly the copy of Luke underwent corrections from Matthew, in many of the numerous cases where they differed from each other; for instance, in the case of the Lord's Prayer. On comparison with Mark, too, Luke might seem the less trustworthy witness, because Mark's Gospel was supposed to go back in substance to Peter himself, that is to the chief eye-witness. But of course the possessors of Matthew and Mark might also note down in their copies the different account or wording given by Luke. The final result of this practice of comparing and correcting or supplementing the Gospels (including even that of John, although that of course had fewest points of similarity) is stated by Jerome (in the preface to his Latin translation of the Gospels) in the following way: "A great mass of error has crept into our copies (the Latin copies, but the case was of course quite the same in the Greek originals of those copies), because the scribes have supplied in one evangelist what another one had more than he, deeming that to be wrongly wanting in the former. Or, where the same sense was rendered in the different Gospels by different words,

the man who had read one evangelist first of the
four, thought that he must correct the others by
that model. So it came to pass that in our copies
everything was mixed together, and that there are
found in Mark many things which belong to Matthew
or Luke, and again in Matthew many belonging to
John or Mark, and likewise in the rest many belonging
to some other of the four." Now, that this mixture
exists in the manuscripts (either Greek or Latin or
Syriac) which have come down to us may be seen
by a look into the apparatus of any large edition.
It would, moreover, be rather incautious to suppose,
that the cases of mixture are to be found in those
editions only under the text and never in the text.
Such implicit trust is not to be placed in any editor,
much less in any scribe; for the idea of the scribes
having possessed the faculty of discerning the genuine
Luke or Mark from the corruptions coming from other
Gospels, would remind us of the legendary Indian
bird, which, out of a pot of milk and water, has the
miraculous gift of drinking the milk and leaving the
water. The case might be different if these interpolations had sprung up about the date of our most
ancient manuscripts; but since their origin is older by
centuries, it is next to impossible that any of our manuscripts entirely escaped their influence. Besides this
kind of corruption of the text, which is the most

general, there must of course have come in, during the same first period, a great many of the ordinary blunders, and although many of these offered themselves to the eye of an attentive reader, who might correct them at once, others of these too remained unobserved. Upon reflection, we must at once feel the absurdity of the supposition (which is nevertheless frequently and even generally made), that ancient readers and the scribes perused the manuscript which they were reading or copying with the careful eye of a thoroughly trained modern critic, attending not only to cases of sheer nonsense, but also to those of awkward or singular expression, and trying by correction to make their text as smooth and pleasing as possible.

Coming now more closely to the object of our examination, we may take first into our hands the Gospel according to St. Matthew. A general consideration, which neglects some few exceptions, shows us that the condition of the text is not much worse than it is in the epistles. Editors have to give generally for Matthew no larger apparatus than for Paul, although the number of different witnesses is far greater than for the latter. But even those witnesses, which elsewhere exhibit a most peculiar character, seem to forego that character as far as Matthew is concerned. I may take for illustration the Latin fragments of the two first Gospels, which hail from Bobbio and are designed by *k*. Mark according to *k* is very different from Mark according to B; but Matthew according to *k*, and Matthew according to B, are very similar. One exception, however, must be made for the Syriac palimpsest from Mount Sinai; there indeed we find in this Gospel also not a few cases of unwarranted shortening, which we may explain by the special condition and origin of this codex, but must disregard here, as leading far away from our theme. But as the other witnesses, including D and Latin versions, exhibit nearly the same Matthew, we may quite safely infer that Western scribes also, and that too in the Gospels, were by no means so utterly careless and lax as they are deemed to be by some eminent modern critics. Scribes who preserved 'Ιωάνης wherever they found it (with a very few exceptions), and wherever they found 'Ιωάννης also preserved it, cannot possibly be termed lax, but rather, if you like, unreflecting or even thoughtless; and so, as a matter of fact, scribes generally were. Western scribes deserve therefore some degree of confidence, as having rendered in sincerity of mind whatever they found or—by distraction of mind—imagined that they found.

Nevertheless there are in Matthew some interpolations in the manuscripts (and consequently some fewer in the printed texts), either of the kind

F

described above or of another kind. In viii. 5 we
read: "And when Jesus was entered into Capernaum,
there came unto Him a centurion," etc. But the
Sinai Syriac MS. and *k* give only: "After that
(μετὰ ταῦτα δὲ) there came unto Him," etc., omitting
the locality. Now, when we compare Luke (vii. 1),
where the same story is told in a partly different
way, we find "He entered into Capernaum," and
may justly suppose that this is one of those cases
described by Jerome, where one evangelist having
something less than another, the former has been
supplied from the latter. Moreover, instead of
ἑκατοντάρχης, *centurio*, the same Syriac witness alone
has χιλίαρχος (the very Greek word in Syriac letters),
that is, *tribunus* (something like "colonel"), and I
am much inclined to regard *centurio* too as a wrong
assimilation, which has extended even to *k*. There
is a corresponding discrepancy between Matthew
(that is the pure text of Matthew) and Luke in the
further course of this narrative. According to Luke
(ver. 8) the *centurio* says of himself that he is "a
man set under authority" (ἄνθρωπος ὑπὸ ἐξουσίαν
τασσόμενος), as befitted a subordinate officer; but in
Matthew that "set" (τασσόμενος) is an interpolation
not found in the majority of MSS., and "under
authority" is to be combined with the following
words "having soldiers under me" (ἔχων ὑπ' ἐμαυτὸν

στρατιώτας), as befits an officer in command; if indeed
we are not to go even further, and to read with the
Syr. Sin., "having authority and soldiers under me"
(ἐξουσίαν ἔχων καὶ στρατιώτας ὑπ' ἐμαυτόν), which
is better Greek and quite unambiguous.[1]

But you will say that if we proceed in this way,
always giving preference to that reading which varies
from the narrative of another Gospel, we are augmenting
difficulties for the establishment of harmony between
the four Gospels. There was a time when theologians
defended the absolute infallibility of the inspired
writers, not only in matters of faith, but also in
matters of fact; but afterwards there came a time
when at least a large part of those of my country
tried to establish the absolute fallibility of the same
writers. If we may credit Professor Harnack, that
time too has passed away; but it cannot be a question
of returning to the former dogma, nor am I writing
for such over-sensitive readers as are apt to take
offence at any shade of alleged discrepancy between
two Gospels. Wherever there are discrepancies, the
reader may choose for himself that variant of the
story which will seem to him most just and most
expressive.

Another kind of apparent interpolation, but from

---

[1] An additional interpolation from Luke vii. 10 is found in some
MSS. (among which the first hand of the Sinaitic ℵ) in ver. 13.

Matthew himself, may be seen in the following
instance. In iii. 2 we read that John the Baptist
was preaching: "Repent ye: for the kingdom of
heaven is at hand"; and in iv. 17 that Jesus preached
exactly in the same words. But the "baptism of
repentance" (Acts xiii. 24; xix. 4) more properly
(I do not say exclusively) belongs to John, and the
case being that not only *k* and the Syriac MSS. of
Cureton and of Mrs. Lewis, but also, as it seems,
Eusebius (*Demonstr. Evang.*, p. 438, cod. P), omit the
"repent ye" (μετανοεῖτε) in the words of Christ, I
think we must read with these witnesses in Matthew
only: "to say that (ὅτι) the kingdom of heaven is
at hand." The actual words of Christ may still
be questioned, because Mark too (i. 15) makes Him
say: "Repent ye, and believe the gospel"; but that
problem is clearly one of another order.[1]

While we had, in these two instances, cases of
what Dr. Hort calls "Western non-interpolation,"[2]
that is where some Western witnesses have remained
free from an interpolation found in the Eastern
authorities: there are, of course, other instances where

[1] Similarly in xx. 16 the words, "For many be called, but few
chosen," are inserted in the majority of MSS., words which are
in their place in xxii. 14.

[2] See also xxvii. 49, where our best MSS. insert a sentence borrowed
from John xix. 34. Nestle, *Einführung in das Gr. Neue Testament*,
p. 109.

the interpolation has infected only Western (and Syriac) texts. The most conspicuous case in Matthew is after xx. 28. There D and Latin and Syriac witnesses insert a rather long passage, the greater part of which is in sense very similar to Luke xiv. 8 ff., but wholly different in the words; moreover, many of the words, or combinations of the words, are such as are never elsewhere met with in the whole New Testament, viz., δειπνοκλήτωρ, or ἔτι ἄνω, ἔτι κάτω, in the sense of the comparatives ἀνώτερον (or -ω), κατωτέρω Unquestionably this passage is alien to Matthew, and must have been interpolated in a very early period from an unknown source. There are in Matthew two cases more of the same kind. In iii. 15 (baptism of Christ) two old Latin witnesses insert the words: *et cum baptizaretur lumen ingens fulsit de aqua, ita ut timerent omnes qui advenerant.* Now, this is an apocryphal tradition, which is known and acknowledged by Justin, and which, according to Epiphanius, was found in the Gospel of the Ebionites. The other passage has found its way into the *textus receptus*, but the best Alexandrian witnesses and the testimony of Jerome are against it: xvi. 2 ff., "When it is evening, ye say, It will be fair weather: for the sky is red. And in the morning, It will be foul weather to-day: for the sky is red and lowering. Ye can discern the face of the sky; but can ye not discern the signs of the times?"   The tradition in itself may well be authentic, and it finds a close parallel in Luke xii. 54 ff.; but it does not stand here in its right place, since the demand of the Pharisees, that Christ would show them a sign from heaven (ver. 1), finds its answer only in ver. 4: "A wicked and adulterous generation seeketh for a sign," etc., as in the corresponding narrative of Mark (viii. 11 ff.), whilst in Luke the introduction is quite different.

A peculiar interest attaches to some passages of the first chapter, where the various readings are of great dogmatic importance.   The close of the genealogy of Christ (in ver. 16): "And Jacob begat Joseph the husband of Mary, of whom was born Jesus, who is called the Christ," is by two Greek minuscules, and by Latin witnesses (among which k and the Latin part of D, the Greek being lost), given in this way: "And Jacob begat Joseph, to whom being espoused (μνηστευθεῖσα, desponsata) the Virgin Mary bore," etc.   This, indeed, must be a wilful alteration from dogmatic reasons: evidently the expression "the husband (τὸν ἄνδρα) of Mary" had been shocking for those readers who believed Mary's virginity to have been perpetual.   The reading of the Sinaitic Syriac comes very near to this: "And Joseph, to whom was espoused the Virgin Mary, begat Jesus," etc,   We must bear in

mind that for "begat," and "was born," or "bore,"
the Greek verb used by Matthew (also according
to those two minuscules) is the same, and Syriac
too makes use of the same verb for both meanings,
only in different voices; so the difference in the reading
of the Syriac witness, especially when we retranslate it
into Greek, amounts only to the repetition of Joseph,
and to the changing of the participle "espoused," into
" was espoused." Materially this makes a thorough
alteration; but the Syriac scribe is not to be
supposed to have known what he did,[1] since he
contradicts himself by adding "the Virgin," and by
giving the detailed narrative in ver. 18 ff. quite in
the ordinary way, with one exception in ver. 25,
where again Latin testimony is concurrent. Instead
of οὐκ ἐγίνωσκεν αὐτὴν ἕως οὗ ἔτεκεν τὸν υἱὸν αὐτῆς
τὸν πρωτότοκον, the Latin *k* has only: "And she
brought forth a son"; and so the Sinaitic Syriac:
"And she bore to him a son," the word "first-born"
being omitted also by the two best Greek MSS. (B
and א), and by other witnesses besides. The pronoun, "to him," which is not found in the Latin
codex, may seem to point in the same direction as
the Syriac reading in ver. 16 ; but the addition of a

[1] Here I quite agree with Professor Zahn and with F. Graefe, who
treated this critical question very carefully in *Theolog. Studien u.
Kritiken*, 1898, p. 124 f. The Curetonian Syriac MS. has "was
espoused," but inserts " who (bore) " after " Mary."

pronoun to a verb is a very slight thing, and the
main importance of the various reading lies in the
omission of the οὐκ ἐγίνωσκεν αὐτὴν ἕως οὗ, that is,
it lies quite in another direction. Οὐκ ἐγίνωσκεν
αὐτὴν ἕως, etc. It follows that afterwards ἐγίνωσκεν
αὐτήν, and the boast of perpetual virginity is destroyed for Mary. The "first-born" too was very
offensive to readers who adhered to such tenets,
although Jerome in his commentary on Matthew,
while acknowledging the reading, strongly denies that
the consequence of brothers to Christ having existed
is to be drawn from it. But as to the expression
"first-born," it has been not without good reason
argued that it may have crept in from Luke ii. 7,
where it is universally attested. I am well aware
that the οὐκ ἐγίνωσκεν, etc., too, may seem to have
been inserted, as there was possibly some reader
who was anxiously contending for the superhuman
generation of Christ. As a matter of fact there
are some passages in Luke where that tendency is
manifest. Luke was not allowed by some Western
readers to say (ii. 41): "And His parents went
to Jerusalem," but they wrote: "And Joseph and
Mary," etc.; or (ver. 48): "Thy father and I have
sought Thee sorrowing," where they left nothing but
"we sought Thee sorrowing." But in Matthew, as
the variants in vers. 16 and 25 appear to stand

in close relation to each other, and as the tendency of that in ver. 16 is unmistakable, the words οὐκ ἐγίνωσκεν κ.τ.λ., are in my opinion to be retained there. At any rate we clearly see that there have been very ancient readers who did not shrink from wilful alterations of the sacred text, if it did not suit their dogmatic convictions, or if it might give support to opposite tenets. Their reasoning was either simply this: It is impossible that an inspired writer should have written this which is incompatible with truth; or else: It is unsafe to allow people to read these words as they stand, since somebody may understand them in a wrong sense, which will lead him to destruction. We shall find more of this kind of alteration or mutilation in other Gospels.

We may pass now from Matthew to the other evangelists, whose textual condition is indeed very different, both in relation to Matthew and to each other. Setting aside for the present all cases of mutual assimilation, we may state their textual condition as follows. In Mark the words and expressions are very frequently liable to doubt, because of discord among the witnesses; there are besides some cases of addition or omission, which are not to be explained in any ordinary way. John has some evident interpolations, e.g. that in v. 3 f. (not to speak of the section from vii. 53 to

viii. 11, which case is quite peculiar); but besides
these a great many words and clauses are not
universally attested; words and clauses, however,
which generally are without any importance for the
sense. There remains Luke, and in his writings,
including Acts, the discrepancies among the witnesses
become by far the greatest of all. It is true that
if we were allowed wholly to neglect Western
witnesses, the remaining discrepancies would not be
over-great, and we may allow ourselves to neglect
that part of the discrepant evidence for the present,
in order to consider first what remains.

I do not intend to speak of minute matters,
but shall come at once to some very conspicuous
and well-known cases. In ix. 54 ff. we read in
ordinary texts: "And when His disciples James and
John saw this, they said, Lord, wilt Thou that we
command fire to come down from heaven, and
consume them, *even as Elias did*? But He turned,
and rebuked them, *and said, Ye know not what
manner of spirit ye are of*" (or rather: Do you not
know, etc.; the second "you" bears an emphasis,
as the pronoun is there in the Greek text). "*For
the Son of man is not come to destroy men's lives,
but to save them*." Now the words in italics are
omitted by a great number of witnesses, varying
however for the separate parts.

Again, in the narrative of the prayer in Geth-semane (xxii. 39 ff.), there is the same discrepancy among the witnesses in giving or omitting these verses (43 f.): "And there appeared an angel unto Him from heaven, strengthening Him. And being in an agony He prayed more earnestly: and His sweat was as it were great drops of blood falling down to the ground."

Lastly, the words in xxiii. 34: "Then said Jesus, Father, forgive them; for they know not what they do," are far from being unanimously attested, there being among the witnesses omitting them both the Vatic. B and the Cantabrig. D.

So in these three cases, as it seems at first, we have this alternative: either the clauses are genuine, and we must seek for an explanation of their omission, or they are spurious, and we must seek for the reason of their insertion. But no less a person than Bishop Lightfoot denies this alternative. He says:[1] "It seems impossible to believe that these incidents are other than authentic, and the solution will suggest itself that the evangelist himself may have issued two separate editions. This conjecture will be confirmed by observing that

[1] See Lightfoot, *Fresh Revision of English New Testament*, p. 32 (3rd edition). I knew this book first from Dr. Salmon's quoting it in his excellent *Thoughts on the Textual Criticism of the New Testament*, p. 135.

in the second treatise of St. Luke (the Acts)
similar traces of two editions are seen, *e.g.* Acts
xxviii. 16, 29." Now the question suddenly gets a
fresh and quite unexpected interest. Can it be that
we possess, either wholly or partly, two separate
editions of Luke's works? That would indeed be a
very important enrichment of our store of authentic
knowledge. But three (or five) passages are a scanty
material for establishing a fact of this importance,
unless there are actually many more in the Acts
than Lightfoot expressly mentions. As a matter of
fact, there are many more in the Acts, and I myself
have written a great deal on them; but now we are
dealing with three passages of Luke, for which the
theory of two separate editions of Luke's works may
perhaps be the *ultima ratio*, as soon as we clearly
see that any other solution is impossible. But that
has not yet been proved. Moreover, the instances to
be taken from the Acts are dissimilar in this point,
that the Cantabrigiensis D, in the case of the Acts,
enables us to propound such a theory, by constantly
presenting an enlarged form of the book; while as
regards the Gospel, D seems to support the omissions
as much as witness against them, agreeing with
Alexandrian authority in the third passage and in
one-third of the first.

There is yet another marked point of difference.

Lightfoot very justly says that those passages of the Acts "are entirely free from suspicion on the ground that they were inserted to serve any purpose, doctrinal or devotional," and he might have added, that there cannot be any more suspicion that they have been omitted for any such purpose. He could not have said as much regarding the passages of the Gospel. Not inserted for dogmatic purposes, very well; but not omitted for such purposes? On the contrary, the first passage might seem to support Marcionite heresy, the second to ascribe to Christ something unworthy of His divine Majesty, and the third to involve a contradiction with other verses. Let me explain the last case first; the second will not even require elucidation. When Christ prays, of course what He prays is fulfilled. Now He has prayed for those who brought Him to the Cross, that their sin might be pardoned; consequently this sin has been pardoned, and if pardoned, has not been avenged. Yet the same Christ has said (ver. 28): "Daughters of Jerusalem, weep for yourselves, and for your children. For, behold, the days are coming," etc. Whether this argument holds good, I need not discuss, the less so as I deny the minor premiss: Christ has not prayed for the Sanhedrin, but for the soldiers who nailed Him to the Cross; for it is of these that the evangelist is speaking both in the foregoing and in the following words, and not of the high priests. But I say thus much: the passage might be understood in this way, and so this argument might be used.

Again, in the first passage the disciples appeal to the example given by Elias, and Christ rebukes them by indicating that they are of another spirit than that of the prophet, and consequently must not act in the same way. Then there is a difference of spirit between the Old and the New Testament, and Marcionite heresy, maintaining a different God for the former, might be justified from these verses. In order to prevent such dangers, it seemed to some orthodox man better to strike out that part of the narrative which might give offence.

If we accept this explanation, retaining of course the questioned verses in our text, then, you may say, Lightfoot's theory falls to the ground. But this conclusion I deny: there may well be other support for it. If the question of the Acts is to be decided in Lightfoot's sense, that decision will contain for the Gospel too a kind of presumption, compelling us to search the state of things there very thoroughly and carefully. Then we shall see that there is still D with its associates, presenting an innumerable host of various readings, of omissions, of additions, and claiming (which cannot in equity be denied), that these variants be either simply accepted, or explained in a satisfactory way, including Lightfoot's theory. As a matter of fact, that theory ought not to bear Lightfoot's name, although it was he who propounded it first in England; or mine own, although I have written perhaps an hundred times as much in support of it as Lightfoot has; but that of Joannes Clericus, who was by far the first propounder. But in order to get a better insight into the genesis of this theory, we may go still further back, and consider the origin and fate of the Codex D (or Cantabrigiensis, or Bezae) more accurately than we have hitherto done.

CHAPTER VII.

THE QUESTION OF THE DOUBLE TEXT IN
ST. LUKE'S GOSPEL AND IN THE ACTS.

THE Graeco-Latin Codex D of the Gospels and Acts
may be justly termed the greatest literary treasure
which the University of Cambridge possesses. It
came into its possession as early as the year 1581,
being presented to the University by the celebrated
French reformer, Théodore de Bèze, or Beza, who had
acquired it in 1562. Until then it had lain neglected
and ill-treated in a monastery in Lyons, which bore
the name of St. Irenaeus; at last somebody had
carried it off from there and given or sold it to
Beza, in about the same mutilated condition which
it exhibits at present. So much Beza himself tells
us; about the former fate of the MS. there is much
uncertainty,[1] there being a trace of its having been
brought as early as 1546 by a Bishop of Clermont

[1] *See* Scrivener's Introd. p. viii ff.

(which is not far from Lyons) to the council of Trent
(Tridentum), when he proved by it that a certain
Latin reading in St. John's Gospel had for itself a
very old Greek authority; now, as a matter of fact,
D is the only Greek MS. we know of which gives the
passage in the form quoted by the Bishop.[1] About
the same time Robert Stephanus got "from Italy,"
as he says (it might seem from Trent), a collation
of a MS. which he in his edition designs by β, and
which proves from the various readings given by him
to be identical with D. Between the sixteenth
century and the sixth, when the codex appears to
have been written, there is a great gap; nevertheless
we may suppose it to belong originally to some place
in southern France, where, at any rate, the tradition
of a text of the Acts similar to that in D has continued down to a very late age. Now, why did Beza
give it to the University of Cambridge? This he
himself declared in the epistle accompanying his
present, stating that the precious codex would be
best preserved there, but "preserved," as he says,
"not published." Why not published too? Because
he was afraid that the very numerous and important
variants, which the codex presented "especially in

---

[1] John xxi. 22, ἐὰν αὐτὸν θέλω μένειν οὕτως ἕως ἔρχομαι. The οὕτως
is given by D alone among Greek MSS.; it might seem to confirm the
more general Latin rendering sic (instead of si) volo eum manere, etc.

the Gospel according to St. Luke," might give offence
to persons who required for their faith a quite established and, so to say, infallible text of the Holy
Scriptures. Nevertheless, Beza himself has published
in his editions of the New Testament at least some
of the variants, and others came into general notice
by-and-by, until as late as 1793 the first edition
of D was made by Thom. Kipling, in a careful and
sumptuous way for those times, although the later
edition by F. G. Scrivener (1864), if less sumptuous,
is more accurate and trustworthy, and now we are
to have an edition which is accurate in the utmost
degree, the codex being *"lucis auxilio in lucem emissus."*
But before any of these editions, those variants in
Luke's works which had become known from D suggested the idea that Luke must have edited them
twice. Joannes Clericus (Jean Leclerc), born in Geneva
in 1657, but living in Holland and belonging to
the Dutch school of philologists contemporary with
the great Bentley, is said by the German theologian
Semler to have published, but under the assumed
name of Critobulus Hierapolitanus, the opinion that
Luke had made two editions of the Acts.[1]   It seems

---

[1] *See* Semler, *J. J. Wetstenii libelli ad crisin atque interpret. N. T.*
(Halle, 1766), p. 8 : *Clericus iam olim, nomine Critobuli Hierapolitani
usus, fere fuit in hac sententia, Lucam bis edidisse Actus. Nec
Hemsterhusius alienus fuit ab hac sententia, forte bis Apostolos
quaedam scripsisse.*

that the opinion, which he did not venture to give under his own name, would have been liable in those times to the charge of gross heresy, and this is indeed very likely, since the Holy Ghost, who was believed to be the real author of Holy Scripture, could not possibly be supposed to have corrected Himself. But for this overstrained dogma, I should think that more scholars than Clericus and Hemsterhusius (whom Semler relates to have been of a similar opinion, viz., that the apostles had written some parts of their work twice) must have hit on that very simple solution.

In cases of wide discordance among witnesses, who seem to be upon the whole equally trustworthy, it may very easily be supposed that the thing itself which their evidence relates to is actually not the same, and if this rule is followed in New Testament criticism, we come at once to the hypothesis of more than one original text. In our day the charge of heresy on account of such an opinion no longer threatens us, though there may be other impediments against the acceptance of a two-edition theory. Accordingly, old Luke appears like one of ourselves, who are used to publish the same book as many times as possible, and if we are diligent, to introduce into it each time more or less correction of style and matter. But what a distance is there

between us and Luke! Of course there is a
world-wide distance between Luke and a modern
book of scientific theology; yet in this respect
the distance between Luke's time and our own is
not so very great, since there exists in both
the notion of " edition " (in Greek ἔκδοσις), and the
possibility of more than one edition of one book,
that possibility having become actual in not a few
known and attested cases in antiquity. But if Luke
comes into question, we must indeed acknowledge
for him a somewhat wider distance. He is not to
be supposed to have given his book to a publisher,
as Cicero did to Atticus, in order that the publisher
might make, by means of his copyists, the required
number of copies, and send them to different
parts of the world. Nor is the term " edition,"
properly speaking, to be applied to the different
forms of Luke's work; we ought to speak rather of
copies, which were privately made and privately
given to friends, and from which other copies would
be made for the use of friends of those friends, and
so on. So there is nothing too modern attributed to
the evangelist, but only a thing common in all ages
in which writing has been practised, and literary
works produced. One copy of the Gospel was that
sent to Theophilus; but when Luke afterwards came
to Rome, he would of course be requested by the

Roman Christians, who heard of his having written a Gospel, to give them, too, a copy of it, and he would write out that copy in the course of perhaps a month and give it them. That fresh copy would not exactly agree with the former, for the writer was entirely at liberty to shorten where he liked, or to insert what he thought suitable for these new readers, or to make improvements in style, or what else he chose to do; and he would naturally desire to do something of that kind, as we usually do, when we write the same essay a second time. Likewise the Acts, which were written in Rome, would be given to the Romans first in one copy, and afterwards sent or brought to Theophilus in another different copy. That the copies in every case were again copied, and in that way the work became generally known in two different forms, is obvious. It cannot, therefore, be denied that this hypothesis of two editions or two original copies sufficiently and amply explains the fact that there are even now existing two different forms of each of Luke's books. There is another fact which is explained at the same time, namely, that Luke's case, as I have stated it, is unique among New Testament writers. Each of the epistles was written once and not twice, and the Gospels of Matthew, Mark, and John, however obscure their origin may be, are not to be supposed to have been originally written in more than one place, nor for more than one definite circle of readers. Or, if this assertion seems to be unwarranted, at least I may say that only in Luke's case we can clearly see the reasons for his writing different copies, since he had first been a member of the Church of Antioch, with which he of course continued to maintain relations, and at a later time became a member of that of Rome.

Of course all these *a priori* considerations are not conclusive: we may admit that possibly there have been different copies of Luke's work, which were equally authentic, and consequently different texts with equal authority; but that the possibility has come to actual existence, and that there are still different texts of that description, remains to be proved. Now, I have already intimated that the condition of the Gospel, and that of the Acts, similar as they are, are still different in one essential point. The similarity, to speak of that first, extends to this, that of the two different copies of each one has been written (as we supposed) for the Romans, and was consequently propagated chiefly in the West, and the other was written for Theophilus, whom we suppose to have lived in the East, and propagated there.

But here at once this difference comes in (which

was found out, as I think, by Professor Nestle, earlier than by myself), that the Romans got the later copy of the Gospel and the earlier copy of the Acts, according to the dates of the two books, which we have established in former chapters, and to the course of the author's life. Now, which of the two copies differing in date would be more correct in style? The latter. Which more prolix (which is akin to a lack of correctness)? The former. I at least, from my own books and writings, should infer this much, and I think it is in accordance with general experience. As for the absolute extent of the work, the later edition of a modern work is usually the more extensive one, for which one reason is this, that the subject-matter has become better known to the author, or has been in a larger measure treated by others, whose statements he has either to embody or to combat. But in modern works the circle of readers is the same for both editions; and it would be quite absurd to present to them the same book in a shape not only not enriched, but on the contrary materially reduced. In this respect Luke's case, as we have supposed it, is of an opposite description: the second copy was written for new readers, who did not know the first. I should think that in this case the second copy would not at all be enlarged, but rather abridged, the work becoming somewhat tedious for the author, or at least. losing something of its freshness for him, so that he was naturally disposed to omit many unessential circumstances and details, which he formerly had given. Consequently, we may suppose that the Acts in the Roman, or Western form, exhibits a comparative prolixness in narration, which has been removed, or lessened, in the copy sent to Theophilus, that is in the form commonly known, and that in the Gospel conversely we shall find in the Roman form many abridgments in comparison with the other, which in this case too is the form commonly known. As for correctness and refinement of style (apart from succinctness, which comes under the head already spoken of), it is clear that Roman Christians did not require it in a higher degree than Theophilus, or Theophilus and his fellow-Christians in the East in a higher degree than those in the West; but the author might give heed to that, while writing the later copy, for his own sake, and certainly he would correct errors committed in the first copy.

So in the Western form of the Gospel and of the Acts, we may expect additions to the known text in the Acts, and omissions in the Gospel, and this is actually the case in D and its associates. Now, additions may be tested, whether they are in harmony with the tenor of the narrative or not, and whether their style is congruent with the bulk of the text or shows differences; but omissions of course are not capable of any such testing. It follows that the theory I am propounding is easier to establish for the Acts than for the Gospel, and so I will start from the Acts. But before entering into my proofs, I must briefly discuss some preliminary topics.

Not only might it be asserted, but it has been asserted, that the enlarged text of the Acts as presented by D is the only original one, and that all omissions found in the common text are due to the negligence of copyists. This strong charge against the common text was produced in Germany, as early as 1848, by Pastor Fred. Aug. Bornemann, who published an edition of the Acts exclusively based upon D.[1] His courage and independence of judgment are very praiseworthy, and he was the first to acknowledge the actual superiority of many readings in D to those of the Eastern witnesses; but his charge against the latter has been, and must be, universally rejected as wholly incredible. There are some individual cases where the omission in B, etc., of words given by D may be quite easily explained by chance; but this principle of explaining

[1] Published in Grossenhain (Kingdom of Saxony) and London.

is not nearly sufficient for the great majority of cases, or for the enormous number of them taken as a whole. Therefore the solution given by Bornemann is wholly inadequate, and I do not think that it will ever again be taken up by any scholar.

On the other hand, to impute the divergencies to the license taken by the scribe of D, or to that of its archetype, is not only equally impracticable, but it has become quite impossible. D does not stand alone, but is supported by other witnesses, and among these there are fathers of the Church of the third and even of the second century, so that a large number of variants and additions has been strictly proved to go back to that time. This is chiefly due to the researches of a very careful German scholar, Peter Corssen, who has written a paper on Cyprian's text of the Acts,[1] showing that the text in which Cyprian read the book was much like D; or, to speak even more exactly, that the Latin version Cyprian made use of was the same of which large fragments have come down to us in some palimpsest leaves from a French codex, called Floriacensis because it came from the monastery of Fleury. These fragments have been published with great accuracy by

[1] See P. Corssen, "Der cyprianische Text der Acta Ap.," in the Program of the Gymnasium of Schöneberg-Berlin W., 1892.

Professor Samuel Berger,[1] and exhibit in their text the nearest affinity to D. Corssen has also proved that St. Augustin, at a certain period of his life (when he wrote those of his treatises which are directed against Manichaeism), used the same Latin version of the Acts, which is the more valuable for us, as he gives in those treatises the whole first chapter of the Acts and a part of the second according to that version, parts which are not contained in the Fleury fragments. Irenaeus too had a text somewhat similar to D, and he enables us to trace back this form of the Acts (which I have denoted by β or by R(omana), in opposition to a, or to A(ntiochena), as far as the end of the second century. It is well known that we have very little of Irenaeus in the original Greek, but read the greatest part of his extant work in an old and careful Latin version. Tertullian's quotations of the Acts are extremely few, but nevertheless he too is proved by them to have used a text of the same condition as that of Irenaeus.

Thirdly, it is now an acknowledged fact (established principally by Corssen), that in D we have not the form β (or R) in its purity, but in a state of frequent mixture and "conflation" with a (A). As I have

[1] S. Berger, *Le palimpseste de Fleury*, Paris, 1889. The first editor of these fragments had been J. Belsheim (*Appendix Epistolarum Paulinarum*, etc., 1887).

already spoken at length of the general practice of comparing manuscripts and correcting the one by means of the other, it cannot be astonishing that in the case of the Acts this same practice has given as a result a conflation of the two texts α and β not only in D, but also (of course in each MS. in a distinct way) in other Greek and Latin MSS., and among them that used by Irenaeus, and those used by Augustine at other periods and for other writings. The thing is quite clearly to be seen in the actual state of D. That MS. has undergone corrections by many persons and at different times, but never (as it seems) systematically, only sporadically, by which the β text has in many places been abolished, and the α text introduced. We are justified in supposing that the archetype of D was in the same condition, there having been introduced, by correction, many readings of the α text, which were of course transcribed by the copyist of D. In many instances the actual reading in D is an impossible mixture of two texts, the correction having been but partly made, or partly transcribed. In order to restore the β text to its integrity, as far as possible, we must therefore have recourse to other witnesses, the more so as no small part of the book, especially that from xxii. 29 to the end, is not extant at all in D, because of the mutilations of that MS. Now, the fragments

of Fleury, together with the quotations in Cyprian
and Augustin, help us a good deal, and that Latin
text seems to be nearly (not altogether) free from
conflation. A third witness for β is a Syriac version,
called the Philoxeniana, or Syrus posterior, in opposition to the older version, the Peshittâ. This
version was collated in the year 616, by one Thomas
(who had been bishop of Hierapolis or Mabbogh, in
Syria, but having been exiled lived near Alexandria),
with some Greek Alexandrian MSS., and the variants
found in those MSS. have been added to the Syriac
text. The Greek MS. used by him for the Acts
was very similar to D, and we see by this fact that
the β text had not been strictly confined to the West,
but had found its way also to the East, a fact which
is confirmed in the case of the Acts as well as in
that of Luke's Gospel by other evidence, and has in
itself nothing astonishing, if we regard the constant
commercial intercourse between Rome and Alexandria. This Greek MS. of the Acts, which has been
preserved to us in this indirect way, may be supposed to have been very ancient, since Thomas
would of course select for his work among the
many copies extant in Alexandria the very oldest,
as seeming to him for that reason the most trustworthy. But it would be an unwarranted supposition
that this MS. exhibited the pure β text without any

conflation, as it is evident that Alexandria was least of all the place where this form of the text would remain free from contact with the other.

I give a brief account of other witnesses: the Graeco-Latin Laudianus (E), preserved in Oxford, written towards the end of the sixth century, and very likely used by Beda Venerabilis, but much inferior to D in purity; the minuscule codex 137 in Milan, useful especially for the last chapters where D is deficient; the Latin Gigas in Stockholm, giving a version which was previously used by Lucifer, bishop of Cagliari in Sardinia († 371); another Latin MS. recently published by Professor Berger, and partly by myself;[1] lastly, one of the old Egyptian versions, commonly called Sahidica. The β text is in all these witnesses much more mixed with a than is the case in D or in the Floriacensis; but we are compelled to gather our evidence from all sides, since even our best witnesses are not wholly free from mixture, besides being so sadly incomplete.

When we now come, after all these preliminaries, to the testing of the β readings, we find the state of things considerably changed. Instead of one single

---

[1] See Sam. Berger, *Un ancien texte Latin des Actes des Apôtres, retrouvé dans un* MS. *provenant de Perpignan, Notices et extraits des* MS. t. xxxv. 1re *partie*, Paris, 1895, and my second edition of the Acts (Leipzig, 1896), p. xxv.

witness of the sixth century, originating probably from Gaul, we have before us a coherent mass of evidence, produced not only by the whole West but also by a part of the East, and going back as far as to the end of the second century. Of the two contending texts the one has for itself the large bulk of witnesses, while the other has still very few; but in point of authority the parties are pretty well matched. There is Cyprian for β; well, but there is Origen for a. Irenaeus and Tertullian are more favourable to β, but Clement of Alexandria stands on the other side. But, you will say, we must not revoke the final decision given by the Church, which has voted for a. That was because it wanted to have one text and not two texts, and preferred of course that accredited by those countries where Christianity had sprung up; we have in fact just now mis-stated the question, speaking simply of two contending parties. The real question is not, which of the two is the original text? but, has a a claim to be the only original text? We are not in the situation of the ancient Church: we, or at least many of us, would prefer to possess, if possible, two original texts completing and explaining each other. So the decision of the ancient Church counts for nothing, and we are called to decide on a *causa integra*. We must put aside all prejudices, and examine the

question as if neither of the parties was beforehand
known to us.   This may be difficult, but it is the
only way of coming to an equitable and unbiassed
decision.

CHAPTER VIII.

THE PROOFS FOR TWO DISTINCT TEXTS IN THE ACTS.

THE first test of β will be that of language, because in this part of the question we have to deal with facts which are in some degree incapable of being differently apprehended, or differently stated. If the claim of β is just, the language in the additions and generally in the variants of β must be proved to be Lucan. If this proof fails, the claims of β will be hopeless; if it succeeds, they will have advanced a good deal on the way to being satisfactorily established.

But you will perhaps object to the question being put in this way. Is there a definite style which may be recognized as that of St. Luke? There is most certainly such a style, pervading both the Gospel and the Acts, and recognizable everywhere. Luke has, indeed, a very wide range in his choice of words, and in almost every chapter he uses words

H

and expressions to which he does not recur again; but on the other hand, he has also his familiar words and ways of speaking, and if anybody questions his authorship of the whole Acts, that doubt will be utterly removed (and has been removed) by the test of the language. So we may safely place entire confidence in that same test in the case of the additions in β.

I shall be as brief as possible in the following analysis of the style of Acts β, referring those readers who want more information to my two editions of the book and to my edition of Luke's Gospel.[1] Here are some simple facts. (1) Number of words occurring in Acts β and nowhere else in the New Testament, 30. (2) Words restricted to Acts β and Luke's Gospel, 3. (3) Words in Acts β recurring in other parts of the New Testament, but not in Luke (Gospel and Acts α), 20. (4) Words occurring in Acts β as well as in other parts of the New Testament, and at the same time in Luke's Gospel, 10. All the four categories have this in common, that the words in question are alien to Acts α; but it is evident that for proving the spuriousness of β (2) and (4) are of no use, be-

---

[1] *See* the index of the words occurring in the Acts at the close of my larger edition, and the summary statistics in my edition of Luke's Gospel on p. xxvii f.

cause those words are warranted by the Gospel. In (1) and (3), taken together, the number amounts to 50, among which are these astonishing enrichments of Luke's vocabulary: πέμπτος the fifth, ἕβδομος the seventh, διάκονος the minister (while Luke has elsewhere διακονῶ and διακονία), ἐξορκίζω, exorcise (while there is ἐξορκιστής elsewhere in Luke). Of course all the fifty ἅπαξ λεγόμενα are not so ridiculous. But now I shall compare the instances for each of the three first categories as they are found in the whole Acts, according to α. (1) 410, (2) 53, (3) 394. The fourth category, which would contain the words used alike in Acts, and Gospel, and elsewhere, cannot be taken into consideration. So the relative proportions are: 410/30, 53/3, 394/20, much alike in the three cases. Now, what proportion of sentences and particles exclusively belongs to β as compared to the rest of the Acts (which is common to α and β)? As I have stated by a simple counting of the words on three pages of my edition, about that of 86 to 530. Then we should expect much more than 50 ἅπαξ λεγόμενα in β. As a matter of fact I am sure that there were more, but the peculiar readings of β are partly preserved to us not in Greek, but in Latin or Syriac, and the words contained in these latter portions are of course excluded from my statistics.

This is not the only way of testing by means of the language, or the best either. The best would be to take every separate addition or peculiar reading in β, and compare it, word for word, with the other writings of Luke. But how can I do that here? I may give one instance as an illustration. Acts x. 25 D makes this insertion: προσεγγίζοντος δὲ τοῦ Πέτρου εἰς τὴν Καισάρειαν, προδραμὼν εἷς τῶν δούλων διεσάφησεν παραγεγονέναι αὐτόν, and then goes on in this way: ὁ δὲ Κορνήλιος ἐκπηδήσας καὶ (συναντήσας κ.τ.λ., as in α). Προσεγγίζειν is new in Luke (one of the fifty words), but he frequently uses ἐγγίζειν, cf. x. 9, ὁδοιπορούντων ἐκείνων καὶ τῇ πόλει ἐγγιζόντων, ix. 3, xxii. 6; see further Gospel, xviii. 35, ἐν τῷ ἐγγίζειν αὐτὸν εἰς Ἱεριχώ; xix. 29, xxiv. 28. Still you insist on the πρός, as making a difference. Well, I may give you a reason for that too: the point of view of the narrator, according to the words immediately preceding, is Cornelius' house; therefore the πρός here comes in, while it is omitted where the place approached is not that of the foregoing narrative, which is the case in the other passages referred to. Προδραμών, see Gospel, xix. 4. Εἷς τῶν δούλων, like Gospel, xv. 26, ἕνα τῶν παίδων, etc.[1] Διεσάφησεν:

---

[1] Weiss (see below) goes as far as to question the Lucan correctness of δούλων, because in ver. 7 οἰκετῶν is used of the same persons.

another of the fifty words, occurring besides once or twice in Matthew. Παραγεγονέναι : παραγίνεσθαι is found in Luke more than three times as often as in the other New Testament writers altogether. Ἐκπηδήσας, see xiv. 14. Are you content now ? Not yet, because of the διασαφεῖν ? Well, I have taken out a sentence containing $\frac{1}{25}$ of all the ἅπαξ λεγόμενα ; of course I might have chosen many and many other sentences without any ἅπαξ λεγόμενον. Then I shall give you an index of the compounds with διά occurring but once in Luke, and most of them but once in the New Testament. *Διαβάλλειν (the asterisk denotes ἅπ. λεγ. in the New Testament), διαβλέπειν, *διαγνωρίζειν? (l. d. Gospel, ii. 17), *διαγρηγορεῖν, διαδέχεσθαι, διαιρεῖν, διακαθαρίζειν, *διακατελέγχεσθαι, *διακούειν, *διαλείπειν, *διαλύειν ? (l. d. Acts v. 36), *διαμάχεσθαι, *διανέμειν, *διανεύειν, *διανυκτερεύειν, *διανύειν, *διαπλεῖν, *διαπραγματεύεσθαι, *διασείειν, διασπᾶν, διαστέλλεσθαι, *διατελεῖν, *διαφεύγειν, διαφθείρειν (*διαφυλάττειν in an Old Testament passage), *διαχλευάζειν, *διαχωρίζεσθαι, διεγείρειν, *διενθυμεῖσθαι, (*διεξέρχεσθαι, l. d. Acts

And yet Luke uses οἰκέτης only twice (see Gospel, xvi. 13), but δοῦλος (in the proper sense) 26 times. Likewise Weiss questions the word immediately preceding (in ver. 24) περιέμενεν, because it stands without an object. Now, the rule of Luke's using this verb *with* an object is based upon *one* instance, i. 4, which is the only other instance of this verb in the New Testament.

xxviii. 3), * διερωτᾶν, διορύσσειν. Does the ἅπαξ
λεγόμενον διασαφεῖν now seem to you sufficiently
warranted for Luke by these 28 other ἅπαξ λεγόμενα
of the same kind (verbal compounds with διά) occurring
in his writings ?

I stated above as one of the features in Luke's style,
that he frequently introduces new words, very often
without ever recurring to them; if that distinctive
feature failed to be found in β, this would be a
strong argument for my opponents, since the imitator
of course would not use any words but those found
in his model.   As it is, I, for my part, give my
verdict for absolute identity of style between β
and α; whoever is still of a different opinion must
take the additions in β one by one, and then take
his concordance and compare, and he will come to
the same results—of course, only if he inquires
without prejudice; in the opposite case, he may
come to any result he likes, and persuade himself
and perhaps others that it is next to impossible
that Luke should have written προσεγγίζειν in this
one case, or that he should have used διασαφεῖν
and never σαφεῖν (which indeed does not exist), nor
σαφής, nor σαφήνεια, nor ἀσαφής, etc.

Let us now see what is to be inferred from
these facts.   In the first place, the spuriousness
of β cannot be shown in this way.   Next, its

genuineness becomes at least highly probable, for identity of language presupposes either a common author, or a model and a very skilful and careful imitator, or two such imitators of the same model. But it is extremely unlikely that there was in any age a man who took Luke for his model in order to interpolate Luke. Perhaps you will say, that somebody who was thoroughly familiarized with Luke's style would quite naturally and not designedly give his explanations of the author's text in the author's own language. It cannot be denied, that in individual cases something like this might happen; for instance, we find in the section on the adulteress, which certainly did not originally form a part of John, a few peculiarities of John's style introduced by copyists: ἕκαστος δὲ τῶν Ἰουδαίων, viii. 9, instead of οἱ δὲ ἀκούσαντες, and ver. 6, τοῦτο δὲ ἔλεγον πειράζοντες in most MSS., as it stands in John vi. 6. But what might happen in a few cases, cannot therefore be supposed to have happened throughout a book; the interpolator, if familiar with Luke's language, did not cease to be still more familiar with his own, and would give many more samples of that than of the author's language.

And now for the second test, that of the matter and of the facts contained in the additions. Can it be rationally supposed that an interpolator rightly understood all the text, without exception ? Certainly not in the case of the Acts, which offer so many difficulties to our understanding. We have seen that no less a man than Eusebius thoroughly misunderstood the proem in the Gospel. Secondly, can it be supposed that the interpolator had any knowledge of the story told, independent of the Acts ? I do not say of the main points, but of the minute detail, that which we have to deal with here ? Evidently this is next to impossible, and barely possible only if the interpolator was a contemporary and a witness of the facts. Now any ordinary interpolator would betray himself by a number of misunderstandings (the book being of such extent), and by a great many wrong statements, which might be refuted by other passages and by our independent knowledge. I may safely say that both Professor Ramsay and Peter Corssen, who have used all their knowledge and skill in order to detect such cases, have completely failed in their attempt. As I have elsewhere answered these highly esteemed scholars,[1] I shall not repeat things formerly said, but prefer to speak at once of the most recent attempt, made by Professor Bernhard

[1] *See* in my second edition of the Acts, on p. viii, and my edition of Luke on p. xxiv ff. (against Corssen, who has given a very careful review of my former edition of the Acts in *Götting. Gelehrte Anzeigen*, 1896, p. 425-448).

Weiss, a veteran scholar in the whole province of New Testament inquiry.[1] It is not from the historical point of view that Professor Weiss contends against D—for he is still disposed to confine himself to that one witness, waiving the rest of the host as much as possible —but from that of textual criticism; he imagines a blundering interpolator, who perverted what he did not understand. Let us take, as an instance of Weiss's handling of the matter, the beginning of xiv., and patiently enter for once into all the minutiae. The English text is in ver. 1 ff.: "And it came to pass in Iconium, that they (Paul and Barnabas) went . . . into the synagogue of the Jews, and so spake, that a great multitude, both of the Jews and also of the Greeks believed. (2) But the unbelieving Jews stirred up the Gentiles, and made their minds evil affected against the brethren." Then follows in ver. 3: "Long time therefore abode they speaking boldly in the Lord," etc. Now, I say that this narrative wants coherence; the result of the action stated in ver. 2 is not given at all. Turning to the Greek, we find that there are in ver. 2 the aorists ἐπήγειραν and ἐκάκωσαν, which oppose the idea of an unsuccessful attempt (imperf.). On the other hand, D and Syr. post. give a quite clear and coherent narrative (ver. 2): "But the

---

[1] B. Weiss, *Der Codex D in der Apostelgeschichte*, Leipzig, 1897.

chiefs of the synagogue of the Jews and their
magistrates directed a persecution against the just,
and made the minds of the Gentiles evil affected
against the brethren; but the Lord soon gave peace.
(3) Long time therefore," etc.   I myself and Professor
Hilgenfeld, Provost Salmon and others, are quite
convinced of the superiority of β in this instance;
and the only difficulty remaining is this, that Luke,
if he wrote β first and then α, must be said not
only not to have corrected his first form, but to
have made it worse.

   We shall have, of course, to revert to this objection; but let us first hear Weiss: "The things
which came to pass in Iconium were entangled by
the interpolator, because he did not understand
the ἀπειθήσαντες Ἰουδαῖοι in ver. 2."   What?   Was
there ever a man who, after the statement in ver. 1,
did not understand οἱ δὲ ἀπειθήσαντες in 2?   "the
unbelieving Jews" after "a great multitude of
Jews believed"?   Are suppositions like this to be
considered justifiable?   "Nor did he understand
ἐπήγειραν, which he supposed to want an object,
not seeing that that verb had an object in common
with the following ἐκάκωσαν, namely τὰς ψυχὰς τῶν
ἐθνῶν."   Here the words in α are really not easy to
understand.   Even if ἐπήγειραν τὰς ψυχάς may be
compared with LXX. (1 Chron. v. 28), ἐπήγειρεν ὁ

ϑεὸς τὸ πνεῦμα Φαλὼχ βασιλέως 'Ασσούρ, still there is the important difference that in that passage there comes a continuation : καὶ μετῴκισεν τὸν 'Ρουβήν (="to do this"), while in the Acts that continuation is wholly wanting, and there it is said as it were only that "they made them," without the necessary complement "do something." But as Weiss does not seem to see any difficulty, we may pass on with him. "So he makes the chiefs of the synagogue as early as that time direct a persecution κατὰ τῶν δικαίων; besides he adds quite superfluously, τῶν 'Ιουδαίων, which is but an 'echo' of the 'Ιουδαῖοι in ver. 1." By no means : as the Greeks ('Ελλήνων) had come in between 'Ιουδαῖοι and ἀρχισυνάγωγοι, the addition was very necessary. But whence did he get his chiefs of the synagogue ? whence his ἄρχοντες ? Not a word on that. And yet the accurate distinction between ἀρχισυνάγωγοι and ἄρχοντες, which has been shown by Professor Ramsay to be quite correct for that time, while it would not have been so for a later one,[1] seems to demand some explanation. Are we to suppose that the same person was at once so stupid as not to understand "un-

[1] See Ramsay in *Church in the Roman Empire*, p. 46, and in *Expositor*, 1895, p. 212 ff. I may notice that D inserts τῆς συναγωγῆς after ἄρχοντες (which has led Prof. R. into some error), but the Syrus post. rightly omits the words. (See also F. H. Fisher, of Pretoria, South Africa, in *Expository Times*, August, 1897, p. 524.)

believing Jews," and yet so fully supplied with
intimate knowledge as to give these details? " In
this way the clause, 'and made the minds of the
Gentiles evil affected,' etc., becomes discordant with
the preceding one: for if the Jews themselves had
been able to direct a persecution against the Christians,
they did not want the assistance of the Gentiles."
I think my readers will answer, that as the power
of the Jewish magistrates did not extend to Gentile
Christians, or to Paul and Barnabas, the assistance
of the Pagan populace and of the magistrates of the
town was on the contrary much wanted.   Besides,
who are the δίκαιοι in β? who the ἀδελφοί in β and α?
" The δίκαιοι are those Jews who had become believers,"
says Weiss.   Quite right; then τῶν ἀδελφῶν, which
word must be of a different meaning (else we should
have κατ' αὐτῶν), will embrace the whole congregation
of Christians (and of course the foreign apostles too),
and quite pertinently, as the hostility of Gentiles
would be at once more excited and more spontaneously
directed against their countrymen than against the
Christian Jews, who were to some extent under the
control of Jewish magistrates.   " He makes this persecution rapidly pass away by the Divine assistance;
one does not, however, see how."   But I do not see
how without some such thing the apostles could
have as much as remained in Iconium, not to say

"have been speaking boldly in the Lord" (ver. 3); they would have been expelled by the combined force of Jews and Gentiles, as they had been from Antioch before. For, according to ver. 2, the hostility of the Gentiles had been actually excited (aor.), and of course against the foreigners and their Greek adherents, while the belief of any of the Jews was for them, as for Gallio (Acts xviii. 15), a matter of utter unimportance.

Professor Weiss continues in this way chapter after chapter; were I to follow him, I should only weary my readers. Besides, I am not writing on the Acts, but on the Gospels. So I may leave readers to study this matter for themselves, giving them for assistance a little book by another German professor, Joh. Belser, who, although a Roman Catholic, nevertheless, as an Englishman writes to me, "is very free from prejudice, and full of good points."[1] He is free also from the dust of minute textual criticism, which in Weiss's book is found from the very beginning, overspreading everything else, and overclouding the main problems, which, if they are to be rightly decided, must be kept clear from minute encumbrances, like the blunders of the copyists of D, or of those of its predecessors. Let these blunders be stated in any

[1] Joh. Belser, *Beiträge zur Erklärung der Apostelgeschichte*, Freiburg im Breisgau (Herder), 1897.

number, you will by that means not even touch or approach the problem; and Weiss, by using that method, has got nearly as far as to the middle of his book before approaching it.

But the evident superiority of β which I have stated in this passage, and which may equally be found in many others—*see* Belser, or Hilgenfeld, or H. Holtzmann, or Nestle, or Zöckler, or Conybeare, or Rendel Harris, or Provost Salmon[1]—and the corresponding inferiority of α urges me to correct myself on one point, which I never regarded as of importance, but which in the general discussion has come into much prominence.

In the beginning, the form I had given my solution of the problem, was that I took β as it were for Luke's rough draught, and α for the corrected and final copy. It is evident that this is not at all essential for the theory which requires merely one older copy and one more recent, and besides it cannot be applied to the Gospel, where Theophilus' copy is the older one, and the Roman copy the later; and

---

[1] *See* Hilgenfeld in *Berl. Philolog. Wochenschrift*, 1896, No. 43; H. Holtzmann in *Theol. Literaturzeitung*, 1896, No. 3; O. Zöckler in "Die Apostelg. als Gegenstand höherer u. niederer Kritik," in *Greifswalder Studien* (1895), p. 195 ff.; F. Conybeare in *American Journal of Philology*, xvii. 135 ff.; R. Harris in *Four Lectures on the Western Text of the New Testament*, 1894; G. Salmon, *Introduction to the Study of the Books of the New Testament*, 7th edition, p. 592 ff.

consequently neither of them is a rough draught, for such would never be sent to Theophilus. Therefore a better form of the solution is this, that Luke's rough draught was kept by him for himself, and that he made from this two successive copies of each book, the older one following more closely the first sketch, while the later departed from it with more freedom and gave (which is the most prominent feature) very frequently an abridged text. It is by way of abridgment that this deterioration has arisen, as in the passage I was just now speaking of. Instead of ἀρχισυνάγωγοι τῶν Ἰουδαίων καὶ οἱ ἄρχοντες was put ἀπειθήσαντες Ἰουδαῖοι, which is materially the same, but in fewer words and in a less definite form ; instead of ἐπήγαγον διωγμὸν κατὰ τῶν δικαίων he simply wrote ἐπήγειραν, using the same word which he had used a little before, xiii. 50 ; then he left out the whole clause ὁ δὲ κύριος κ.τ.λ., and because of the omissions in 2 f. altered the words in ver. 4 and those in 5 (as they are given by the Syrian witness), writing in 4 ἐσχίσθη instead of ἦν ἐσχισμένον, and so on. Likewise in x. 25 (the passage of which we analyzed the words) the text in α sprang out of that in β by mere abridgment. Whether Luke is to be blamed, as a writer, because of these omissions and abridgments, is a question which I need not discuss here ; perhaps he is, from our point of view : but he might answer with Euripides : τί δ' αἰσχρόν, ἢν μὴ τοῖσι χρωμένοις (to Theophilus) δοκῇ ? At the same time, by changing the form of our hypothesis in this way, we get a full explanation of the converse cases, which, if much rarer, are nevertheless not wholly absent even from the Acts, viz., those, where α gives something more than β.[1] In these, Luke's archetype, or rough draught, has been preserved in the later copy, as would of course happen now and then, from respect to the peculiar circle of readers addressed, or by mere chance, just as in our own writing and copying.

What I have just said is also fitted to meet, in some measure, the objections raised to my theory by Mr. T. E. Page (see *Classical Review*, July, 1897). On the whole, he treats it somewhat contemptuously, saying that the question of the origin of the β variants may occupy the attention of scholars " *with ample leisure.*" I am very much afraid he does not include himself in that number. If he had given some leisure hours to the individual problems he touched, he would, *e.g.* have found in Provost Salmon's review of my edition (see *Hermathena*, vol. ix. p. 235) a very judicious appreciation of the passage in xxi. 16. Readers of the common text are almost of necessity led to the erroneous opinion that Mnason, who is

[1] *See* my edition of Luke, pp. v f., xxvi, xxxiv f.

mentioned there, was living in Jerusalem, while
from the β text there comes the clear statement
that he lived in a village mid-way between Jerusalem
and Caesarea. "Anybody," says Mr. Page, "could
make these corrections." Certainly, anybody, who
was very attentive, and reflected a good deal, and
compared other passages, and had no small amount
of ingenuity: that is to say, *not* "anybody." The
most striking piece of reflection of that "somebody"
has been put into due light by Provost Salmon. As
Mnason is said to have been an *old* disciple, the
result is that, by giving him this dwelling-place,
a connection is established between this passage and
that in xi. 2, where Peter is said to have preached
the Gospel in the villages through which he passed
in going up from Caesarea to Jerusalem. "It is
a natural combination," says Salmon, "that Mnason
was one of his converts." And for that fine combination we are under obligation to somebody, who
must have been anybody except Luke. Why not
Luke? Because Luke, if he had written first the
sentence as it stands in β, never would have brought
it into that obscure form in α? Then I answer,
that he did it for abridgment's sake; for the unknown
village where Paul slept for a single night is a matter
of infinite unimportance, as Mr. Page says. No, I
do not say that, Mr. Page will answer: at whose

I

house he slept in a village is unimportant; but
Luke does tell us that he received kindly hospitality
from Mnason in Jerusalem, and the corrector has
quite misunderstood the real meaning. Impossible,
I reply, for it must "seem very strange to us that
Paul should have been dependent on a stranger
for entertainment at Jerusalem, a place where we
should have supposed he could have relied on the
hospitality of private friends" (Salmon), and that
in order to introduce Paul to Mnason, whose house
he might find himself, the disciples of Caesarea
should have accompanied him on that long journey.
The accompanying, on the other hand, was quite
natural, if Mnason lived in a village known to those
disciples, but not known to Paul.[1] The aorist
ξενισθῶμεν too, denoting an action of some definite
time, makes very strongly against this interpretation
of the a text: if the sojourn in Jerusalem was
spoken of, we ought to have ξενιζώμεθα. But Luke,
Mr. Page might reply, makes a wrong use of the

[1] Here B. Weiss (p. 101) comes to the assistance of Mr. P.,
saying that it was not for Paul's sake, but for his large company
of uncircumcised men, that the accommodation in Jerusalem was
procured in this cumbrous way. But on Paul's former visit (Acts
xv.) there had also been at least one uncircumcised man (Titus)
in his company, who had of course found accommodation, and
on that same occasion the equal rights of uncircumcised Christians
had been formally recognized by the whole congregation of
Jerusalem.

aorist also in xxviii. 14, ἤλθαμεν (a passage to which my reviewer actually refers). Wrong only in so far as the result is given beforehand, and nevertheless the author, in the next verse, returns to things which had occurred during the journey. In xxi. 18 there is nothing of this kind, as the author correctly says in 15: ἀνεβαίνομεν εἰς Ἱεροσόλυμα, and 17: γενομένων δὲ ἡμῶν εἰς Ἱεροσόλυμα; συνῆλθον, which is used of the disciples in 16, seems to imply that from the village they returned to Caesarea.

There are two passages in β which deserve our particular notice, because of their bearing either upon the author or on his former book. In xi. 27, after the mention of the prophets who came from Jerusalem to Antioch, β inserts: "and there was a great joy. And we being assembled, one of them, named Agabus," etc. Now, this we (συνεστραμμένων δὲ ἡμῶν), which is also attested by St. Augustin, clearly shows that the author was at that time a member of the Church of Antioch, and as the period is so very early, we can hardly doubt that Luke really was a native of Antioch, which is the tradition given by Eusebius (*Hist. Eccl.* iii. 4, 6), and others. Roman Christians cannot have been ignorant of this fact, and the "we" was to them perfectly clear. Besides this, we get by these three words a fresh *we-section*, which is of the greatest importance for showing that the occurrence of the first person, which is found again in xvi., and in xx., etc., can by no means be employed (as theologians have frequently employed it) for the purpose of dissecting the Acts into parts originally independent from each other.[1]

The other passage is that which opens the whole book, and connects it with the Gospel. There D is (as F. Graefe and P. Corssen have shown before me) corrupt by way of conflation, and we are restricted, in Weiss's words, to "Latin" witnesses; in other words, we have the testimony of St. Augustin given in two places, and in the most trustworthy form, the whole chapter having been copied by him. This witness gives the text of ver. 2 as follows : *in die qua Apostolos elegit per spiritum sanctum et praecepit praedicare euangelium.* But, says Weiss, this combination of " to preach " (κηρύσσειν) and " Gospel " (a combination which is here attested also by D and other witnesses) is not Luke's habit; he says (Gospel, viii. 1), κηρύσσων καὶ εὐαγγελιζόμενος. Now, how many times does Luke make use of εὐαγγέλιον ?

---

[1] About this passage Weiss, who has reserved it for the end of his book (p. 111 ff.), does not speak with any confidence, while he, at the same time, judiciously rejects all theories of dissection by means of the "we."

Just twice, Acts xv. 7 (in Peter's speech), and, xx. 24 (in that of Paul); besides him the combination exists in Matthew, and in Mark, and in Paul, and Luke might enrich his language by use of it, if need be, from his teacher Paul. The main point is, that instead of "until the day He was taken up," there has been put in this text *in die qua*, the mention of the ascension of Christ having been wholly suppressed.

As this is the proem of the work, we must consider it very carefully, as we did in a former chapter in the case of the proem of the Gospel. Luke is giving here a summary of his former book; in the α text, he outlines its contents by giving the close, while in this β text he does so by giving the beginning, going on, in the next verses, to sum up the further contents, and inserting in ver. 4, "how" (*et quomodo* $= \kappa a \grave{\iota}$ $\acute{\omega}\varsigma$), in order to indicate that this too was already related in the Gospel, as it actually stands (Gospel, xxiv. 49). At the same time he is giving here some fresh details, especially the forty days in ver. 3, and leads on, in this way, to the more detailed relation of the ascension which is to follow. This text therefore seems to be quite consistent with itself, but yet we are told by Professor Weiss, that it is impossible, because Jesus is stated to have begun His working and teaching on the day (*in die qua*) He chose the Twelve, a fact which is related by Luke as

late as in vi. 13 ff. As this objection is rather
serious, we must try to re-translate the "*in die qua*"
into Greek with more care than I did in my edition,
where I gave it in this Greek expression: ἐν ᾗ
ἡμέρᾳ. But Augustin has not *in qua die*; therefore
why not ἐν ἡμέρᾳ ᾗ? Very well, you will say,
but in this I do not see any real change. Nevertheless, there is a change in the meaning. Ἐν ᾗ
ἡμέρᾳ is the same as ἐν (ἐκείνῃ) τῇ ἡμέρᾳ ᾗ, and
distinctly denotes some definite day; but ἐν ἡμέρᾳ
ᾗ, without the article, presents itself as being like
in sense to the identical LXX. phrase, as we have
it, for instance, in Jer. vii. 22: "For I spake
not unto your fathers, nor commanded them *in
the day that* (ἐν ἡμέρᾳ ᾗ) I brought them out of
the land of Egypt, concerning burnt offerings or
sacrifices." Evidently the ἡμέρα is applied there
not to a single definite day, but in a looser way
to a definite time extending over many days, and
so our Hebrew dictionaries teach us that the corresponding Hebrew word very frequently expresses
the general notion of time. Likewise, our dictionaries
of New Testament Greek tell us that the looser
Hebrew notion of "day" has introduced itself in
many passages, not only in the plural form, but
also in the singular, see John viii. 56; xiv. 20; xvi. 23,
26; Eph. vi. 13; 2 Cor. vi. 2; 2 Pet. iii. 18. So

Luke says, quite in accordance with the facts: *All that Jesus began to do and teach in that time when he chose the twelve*, and the "impossible" reading proves to be quite possible and easy. It is true that Luke elsewhere has either ἐν ἡμέρᾳ ᾗ only of a single but *not* definite day (Ev. xii. 46), or ἐν ἡμέραις αἷς of a definite *time* (ibid. i. 25); but these passages also are both without parallel in Luke; and it is very clear that in that of the Acts he could not employ the plural: ἐν ἡμέραις αἷς ἐξελέξατο κ.τ.λ., because that event had been told in the Gospel as having come to pass on a definite and very memorable day, that of the great Sermon on the Mount.

It may be objected that I am gliding back into the ordinary notion of "day," after having established that here ἡμέρα means "time." But the original notion of the word could never be wholly absent from the mind of the writer, and for that reason a distinction between the plural and the singular is maintained throughout: ἐν ἡμέρᾳ ᾗ ἐπεῖδεν ἀφελεῖν κ.τ.λ. (words of Elizabeth, Ev. i. 25), would have been quite unnatural after: περιέκρυβεν ἑαυτὴν μῆνας πέντε, and so then the plural comes in.[1]

Let us consider now the reading in α, Ὧν ἤρξατο

---

[1] In Gosp. ix. 51 (*see below*), τὰς ἡμέρας τῆς ἀναλήμψεως αὐτοῦ does comprehend the time of the passion, the resurrection, and up to the day of Ascension, which day, however, has no special importance for this passage.

ὁ Ἰησοῦς ποιεῖν τε καὶ διδάσκειν, ἄχρι ἧς ἡμέρας. The
combination of ἤρξατο with ἄχρι may be justified,
in some measure, by other passages, but nevertheless
is rather harsh; and Weiss thinks that readers who
did not understand it have therefore altered "*until*"
to "*in.*" And have left out, he ought to continue,
the Ascension; but he prefers, as we saw, to deal
with D alone, where (by means of conflation) the
Ascension is mentioned, and the rest of the evidence
is nothing to him. I say: readers of the New
Testament must have been accustomed to digest
harder things than this ἤρξατο ἄχρι, and if they did
not understand it, the most simple way was to leave
out the "began." There comes next: ἐντειλάμενος
τοῖς ἀποστόλοις διὰ πνεύματος ἁγίου οὓς ἐξελέξατο
ἀνελήμφθη. The clause is in a very awkward way
complicated by the insertion of οὓς ἐξελέξατο; I
do not think that this can be the original hand of
Luke. But if we suppose the words as they are
in β to represent Luke's first writing, the thing
becomes quite transparent: he has encumbered the
clause in order to bring in the Ascension, without
leaving out the choice of the apostles. And why
did he want the Ascension to be mentioned? Because
the corresponding form of the Gospel (α, or A) closes
with the Ascension; α of the Gospel and α of the
Acts must be made to agree.

Is there then in β of the Gospel any difference on this point? Assuredly there is, and now we are at last returning to Luke's Gospel, on behalf of which we have taken this long circuit through the Acts.

CHAPTER IX.

THE DOUBLE TEXT IN ST. LUKE'S GOSPEL.

It is a fact which has been the subject of much and serious discussion, that at the close of Luke's Gospel the Ascension of Christ is by no means attested by all manuscripts. Besides the known text there is another one, having very good attestation, and therefore received by Tischendorf, as well as by Westcott and Hort: (51) "And it came to pass, while He blessed them, He was parted from them" (without "and carried up into heaven"). "And they" (without "worshipped Him, and") returned to Jerusalem with great joy," etc. If this text is to be accepted as the only original one, and the omitted words are to be rejected as interpolations, the fact of the Ascension of our Lord, which we confess every Sunday, will in the main rest exclusively upon the testimony of the Acts, that of Mark being rejected together with the whole close of his Gospel. But this by the way: I am not writing on dogmatics.

It has been argued, on the other hand, that Luke gives another testimony for the same fact, by saying as early as in ix. 51 : "When the time was approaching that He should be received up" (ἐν τῷ συμπληροῦσθαι τὰς ἡμέρας τῆς ἀναλήμψεως αὐτοῦ), and that by mentioning the Ascension here, he clearly indicates his intention of relating it at its proper place. Moreover, as the reading in ver. 52 : "*they returned to Jerusalem with great joy, and were continually in the temple, praising (and blessing) God,*" is universally attested, the words left out by a part of our witnesses can hardly be supposed to have been originally absent from the narrative. If the apostles had seen their Lord carried up to heaven, there was a reason both for their rejoicing and for their being continually in the temple, that is to say, not expecting any more appearances of Him; but if the appearance related had ended in like manner as the others, this sequel becomes quite incomprehensible.

Why, then, are the words omitted by a part of the witnesses? You ought to ask first: Who, then, are the witnesses upon whose evidence Tischendorf and Westcott-Hort omit the words? There is, in the first place, D, and together with D some Latin versions, and St. Augustin, and the Syriac version[1]

---

[1] The Syriac witness gives, however, a word like ἐπήρθη instead of διέστη or ἀπέστη.

of Mount Sinai, and lastly, but only as regards
the words in ver. 51, the first hand of the Greek
MS. from Mount Sinai (א). Now, the solution of
the enigma is quite near at hand: it is β of the
Gospel which omits these words, while α had them,
and α, in this case, is the earlier copy and represents
more truly Luke's original writing. The other question,
too, *why* the words are left out in β, has already
almost found its answer: it was in order to fit the
close of the Gospel β to the beginning of the Acts
β, and this was recognized ten years ago by the
German pastor, Ferdinand Graefe.[1] Likewise as the
original beginning of the latter book was, in some
way, altered by the author, when writing for Theophilus, in order that it might suit the close of that
form of the Gospel which had been sent to him:
so Luke, when he again copied his Gospel for the
use of the Romans, altered its close with respect
to the beginning of the Roman Acts. It is true
that the last chapter of the Gospel β and the
first of the Acts β do not give a really continuous
narrative; but the discordance, which consists in the
double relation of the Ascension, is at least veiled,
and does not strike the eye of an ordinary reader.
We must suppose therefore that during Luke's first
stay in Rome, at a time when he already contemplated

[1] See *Theologische Studien u. Kritiken*, 1888, iii. p. 522 ff.

the writing of the Acts, or had even fixed the beginning of that book, he wrote out the copy β of
the Gospel. Why, then, did he not submit its last
chapter to a more thorough reconstruction ? I should
think, because he was depending on a written authority, and did not venture to alter overmuch the
account given by him on that authority. Likewise he had a written authority for the first chapter
(or the first twelve chapters) of his Acts, and felt
himself bound to follow that authority very closely.
I am even inclined to think, that the rather rough
form, which the beginning of that book exhibits
even in β, if we compare it with the extremely
refined proem of the Gospel, is due to his following
some written text, which furnished him with the
materials for the first part of the Acts. And here
I may venture to propound a conjecture. Suppose
that Mark was the author who had written a continuation to his Gospel, and that this continuation
fell into Luke's hands at some time after he had
finished his own Gospel. I find that conjecture,
for instance, in Weiss's book on Mark, of course as
a conjecture, not as a certainty ; he thinks it probable that Mark really had closed his Gospel at
xvi. 8, and afterwards wrote a continuation beginning with the appearances, that is to say, the first
actions of the risen Christ, and going on to tell

what the same Christ had done afterwards by means
of His apostles.

Supposing all this, we may well conceive the
beginning of Mark's second book to have been nearly
identical with that of the Acts, with this exception,
that the appearances did not come into the summary
of the earlier book, but were given in detail as a part
of the second. Of course this conjecture cannot be
tested or verified, except perhaps on one point.
Luke, as we have seen, refers his readers to the
memorable day when Jesus elected His apostles,
and to his description thereof in his Gospel, vi.
13 ff. Comparing that passage, we find that the
name of apostles is really there, but that the commission given to those "messengers," viz., to preach
the gospel, is not expressly stated. But when we
turn to the corresponding passage in Mark (iii. 13 ff.),
there we actually find that commission (ver. 14), "that
He might send them forth to preach" (or "to preach
the gospel," after the text in D), and so the curious
fact is noticeable that Luke's summary suits Mark's
narrative even better than his own. We shall return
to that passage in Mark in a later chapter (see x.).

Leaving aside these conjectures for the present, and
returning to the last words of Luke's Gospel, I must
state that the omission of "and was carried," etc.
might be, not without some degree of probability,

ascribed to some reader of Luke, who was offended by the repetition in Acts i. Of course that reader must be sought for in the very first period, when Gospel and Acts still formed as it were one whole; for in after-times, when Luke's Gospel had been combined with the other three, and the Acts with the Catholic epistles, no such offence could be taken. But we have seen that there actually was a time when Luke's works were not yet read separately. So, if the omission of the words in Gospel, xxiv. 51 f. were an isolated fact, we should require no other explanation. But as the beginning of the Acts exhibits a corresponding phenomenon of double-reading, and indeed in a very complex way, which far exceeds the abilities and the possible fancies of ordinary readers, both of these phenomena are to be explained on the same ground, which is sufficient for both; and Graefe himself, who formerly had applied to both the hypothesis of an interpolation, now quite agrees with me in referring the facts to Luke's own treatment of his work.[1]

But my readers will still ask me this question: What does your supposition of a double authentic form of the Gospel rest upon? This one passage in xxiv. 51 f. is a very narrow basis, and you have expressly declined to adopt Bishop Lightfoot's

[1] *Theolog. Studien u. Kritiken*, 1898, p. 137 f.

analogous solution for three other passages; what others have you then? Of course I have plenty of others to which I apply this solution; but I am bound to point out passages to which this solution alone applies. As the difference between D and the commonly adopted text, in the case of the Gospel, consists mainly in omission, the proof for two authentic texts must be much more difficult than in the Acts. But to counterbalance this, the proofs for the very early existence of the Western text are more numerous, and go much further back in the Gospel. I entreat my readers to allow me to give these proofs first of all.

Now, it may be sufficiently established that *Justin* Martyr, who lived in Rome about the middle of the second century, used the β form of Luke's Gospel. But as his quotations are few in number and free in form, and as he always speaks of the Gospel in general, never quoting by name either Luke or Matthew,[1] I shall waive this witness, since I have another of the same time, *Marcion*, the well-known founder of a heretical sect which lasted for a very long time. This man, a native of Sinope on the Black Sea, went to Rome about 138, and

[1] E. Lippelt, an important discovery by whom I have mentioned before, has directed his and my attention to this point also, and will publish his results in due time.

became there the chief of a separate sect about 144. His notion of Christianity was that of an extreme Paulinist, who decidedly rejected all that seemed to retain a flavour of Judaism, not only therefore the whole Old Testament, but also three Gospels out of four, acknowledging only that written by Paul's disciple Luke, and rejecting also the rest of the writings in the New Testament, besides the Pauline epistles. But even in those books which he kept very many sections or verses were struck out by him, as tainted by Judaism, and his Gospel, which of course bore no distinctive name, being his only one, began in a very abrupt way with Christ's coming down to Capernaum (*see* Luke iv. 31). The New Testament of the Marcionites has perished, but not without leaving considerable traces in writings directed against this sect, among which Tertullian's four books against Marcion occupy the first place. It has been attempted, therefore, partly to reconstruct Marcion's New Testament by means of Tertullian and other writers, the most recent and most complete and accurate reconstruction having been made by Professor Theodor Zahn.[1] Now it cannot be doubted that Marcion's text of Luke's Gospel did not exhibit the form commonly known, but that attested by other Western evidence, such as D and

---

[1] *See* Th. Zahn, *Geschichte des N.T. Kanons*, ii. 2, 1, p. 411 ff. (*Marcion's Neues Testament*).

K

Latin versions, and in this way a different Western text of the Gospel is proved to have existed as early as in the first half of the second century.

I might well be content, as regards antiquity of evidence, with this one witness, the rest being of course of a somewhat later age; but I shall name two more, in order to show by them how the Western text spread more and more widely to the different parts of the ancient world. *Tatian*, a Syrian by birth, became a disciple of Justin, probably in Rome, and afterwards went back to his own country, where as it seems he gave to his countrymen the first Gospel in their native tongue, the famous Diatessaron, that is one Gospel made out of four. I am not going to enter into the very intricate questions about Tatian's Diatessaron, but shall content myself with saying this much, that in the few unadulterated remnants of that work there appear clear traces of the Western text of Luke,[1] and that the quadripartite Syriac Gospel, as contained in the MSS. discovered by William Cureton and by Mrs. Lewis, counts as regards a number of passages among the witnesses for the Western text.

A third witness for the same is *Clement* of Alexandria, although neither he, nor Tatian, nor perhaps Marcion, seems to have possessed the Western text

[1] *See* on the Diatessaron, Zahn, *ibid.*, p. 530 ff.

while still in its pure form. Apart from the conflations with other Gospels, which as we have seen began
at a very early date, conflations with the Oriental
text must have been even more inevitable than in
the case of the Acts, because the Gospel was so
much more read and copied and collated than the
Acts. A general survey shows me that the β text
of the Gospel, while more widely spread than that
of the Acts, was in the same measure more conflated
with the other. Clement read the Acts in the α
text, but the Gospel in a mixed one, and so our
chief MSS. of the New Testament, the Vaticanus B
and the Sinaiticus א, which are either of Alexandrian
origin or intimately connected with Alexandrian texts,
follow α in the Acts, and exhibit a mixture of α
and β in the Gospel, more especially א in its first
uncorrected state, while in B there are but a few
passages showing Western influence. We saw however before, that even of the Acts the β text had
spread also to Egypt, and that a MS. existing there
as late as at the beginning of the seventh century
became, by means of the later Syriac version, one
of our best witnesses for Acts β.

I may now go on to test the combined evidence of
all these witnesses, and first as regards the omissions.
In viii. 43 we have in α: "And a woman having an
issue of blood twelve years, which had spent all her

living upon physicians, neither could be healed of
any, came behind Him," etc. D, which is supported
by an old Egyptian version, exhibits the whole relative
clause in five words: " whom no one could heal,"
while B and the Sinaitic Syriac version, together
with the Armenian (which is dependent on Syriac
authority), simply omits " had spent . . . physicians," so that we have "could not" instead of "neither
could." Can there be here any suspicion of interpolation ? I do not think so (although Westcott
and Hort follow B here as elsewhere), for Mark (v.
26), while giving the same thing in substance, differs
entirely in the words, which is the ordinary relation
between the two Gospel-writers in matters which
they have in common. So there can be no doubt
that Luke originally wrote what we read in the bulk
of MSS. Whence, then, the omission ? and whence
the even more abridged form in D ?

Let us take another instance. Chap. x. 41 f., in the
well-known words of our Lord to Martha, there is a very
strong Western evidence for omitting the whole
bulk of them, leaving nothing but: " Martha, Martha,
Mary has chosen the good part, which shall not
be taken away from her." Now, can this in any
possibility be a case of (as Westcott and Hort express
it) Western non-interpolation ? Those editors themselves do not think so, nor is it, on the other hand,

in any way easy to account for the omission of the
words, if they are genuine, except by the theory
of two original texts, one longer and another more
abridged.

Again, in xii. 19 the rich man of the parable,
according to the Western evidence, says nothing
but this: "And I will say to my soul: thou hast
much goods, be merry." This is quite sufficient
for the sense; but everybody, I should think, would
prefer the longer form given in the other text:
"Soul, thou hast much goods laid up for many years;
take thine ease, eat, drink, and be merry." Why
should we suppose ancient copyists or readers to have
had such a different taste, as arbitrarily to mutilate
this fine passage? There was no dogmatic reason
for it whatever, nor any other save mere idleness,
which cannot rationally be thought to have formed
an essential factor in New Testament tradition.
Luke's case, of course, was different; he did not
cherish his own work so much as others were bound
to do.

The account of the colt which Jesus made His
disciples bring Him from the village (xix. 29 ff.),
is by D given in this abridged form: (31) "And
if any man ask you . . . thus shall ye say unto
him: The Lord has need of him. (32) And they . . .
went their way . . . (34) and answered, The Lord

hath need of him. (35) And they brought the colt,
and cast their garments upon him," etc. In this last
verse we must consider the Greek words too:

α

Καὶ ἤγαγον αὐτὸν πρὸς
τὸν Ἰησοῦν, καὶ ἐπιρίψαντες
αὐτῶν τὰ ἱμάτια ἐπὶ τὸν
πῶλον ἐπεβίβασαν τὸν
Ἰησοῦν.

β (D)

Καὶ ἀγαγόντες τὸν πῶλον
ἐπέριψαν τὰ ἱμάτια αὐτῶν
ἐπ᾽ αὐτὸν καὶ ἐπεβίβασαν
τὸν Ἰησοῦν.

You see that Ἰησοῦν stands twice in α, and · the
reason is, that after πρὸς τὸν Ἰησοῦν it was necessary
to bring in τὸν πῶλον, because ἐπ᾽ αὐτὸν would
have been ambiguous, and after that it was again
necessary to repeat Ἰησοῦν. On the other hand,
in β the unnecessary πρὸς τὸν Ἰησοῦν has been
left out and the first clause given by the participle,
and in this way the whole sentence has been brought
into a smoother and more elegant form. Now, if such
transformations are to be ascribed to copyists or
readers, I am afraid we shall get a kind of copyists
or readers who are but the creation of our own fancy,
without having had or having now any existence
in reality. I, for my part, am not able to recognize
here anything but the license of an author, who is
handling his own work, and the skill of a writer.
Speaking generally, the case is the converse of what
we find in a passage of the Acts (xxv. 24 ff.). There

Festus, according to the α text, is made to say thus much: "But when I found that he had committed nothing worthy of death, and that he himself hath appealed to Augustus, I have determined to send him." Of course in reality he said much more than this, stating the case to his illustrious audience in its full length, and in accordance with this we have in β a much more detailed speech, but one in which things are repeated which the author himself had already told. He did quite well to avoid these repetitions when he wrote a second copy. So, in the account of the α Gospel, the things which came to pass are first predicted and prescribed bý Jesus, and next represented for a second time in their fulfilment and execution; that repetition has been avoided in β, and yet not wholly, inasmuch as even the words "and answered, The Lord hath need of him," cannot be deemed to be strictly necessary.

I might give a series of cases of a similar character, the number of omissions in D being infinite, but do not think that this would be in any way profitable. So I refer my readers for further instances to my edition of the β text, with which I think they will be content, and will be likely to ask me this question: Are there then no converse cases of addition in D? There are indeed such cases, just as in α of the Acts, but comparatively

few in number, and some others there are where
neither of the texts has either an addition or an
omission, but the words are different. Let me speak
of these first. There is a personage mentioned by
Luke, who may be unknown to some of my readers,
a man by name Chuzas, steward to Herod the tetrarch
and husband to Joanna, who was one of the women
accompanying Christ (see Luke viii. 3). The name,
of course an Aramaic one, does not occur anywhere
else. Now, if we scrutinize our Latin witnesses very
carefully, we find in *l* (an old Latin version of the
seventh century, existing in Breslau and published
by Professor Haase) instead of *Chuzae*, *Cydiae*. This
is a very ancient Greek name : there was one
Cydias a lyric poet, and another an Attic orator,
mentioned by Aristotle, and another a painter from
the island of Cythnus, and so on. How does the
Latin copyist come by that name ? By chance ?
Impossible. By correction ? Still more impossible.
I say he came by it in the simplest way in
the world, by tradition, which goes back to Luke
himself. That man had two names, one Aramaic
and one Greek, of somewhat similar sound, which
he had adopted as more convenient for the cultivated
and elevated circle in which he lived : just as other
Jews, as early as in the time of the Maccabees, trans-
formed their name of Jesus into Jason, and as

modern German Jews called Aaron prefer to call themselves Arthur. Luke must originally have written : " of Chuza, who was also called Cydias"; but, when copying first for readers in Syria and Palestine, he left out the Greek name, and when copying again for Roman readers, he left out the Aramaic one. There cannot be a more simple solution of a puzzling problem, which, if you attempt in any other way, you will find insoluble.

Now as regards the additions found in D, I think it best to follow the same method of solution which has proved practicable here, as far as it will go. The best known of the additions in D is that in vi. 5 : " On the same day He saw a man working on the Sabbath, and said unto him : Man, if thou knowest what thou art doing, blessed art thou ; but if thou dost not know it, thou art cursed, and a transgressor of the law." I do not see here anything unsuitable to our Lord ; but these words were likely to give great offence even to Christian Jews, because the spirit of the saying is quite that of Paul who, on the one hand, gives us to understand that it is a weakness in faith to esteem one day above another (Rom. xiv. 5 f.), and on the other asserts that nevertheless the man so esteeming is not allowed to act against his own conscience (ibid. 23). It is, therefore, quite credible that Luke preferred to leave out this saying in the form of his Gospel destined for Oriental congregations, a very considerable part of which consisted of Jews, whilst in Rome there was no cogent reason for omitting it.[1] It is very remarkable that for this addition D is the only witness; there is even no trace of Marcion's having known it, and so it seems that it had very early disappeared from Roman copies, and was preserved only in Gallic ones, which may have been derived (if I am allowed to make a rather bold conjecture, without laying any stress upon it) from an ancient copy carried by Crescens (2 Tim. iv. 10) to Gaul. For that there were written Gospels at that time within the reach of an evangelist like Crescens, and that every evangelist undertaking a mission in a new country took care to provide himself with a written Gospel, is for me a thing beyond question. But why did

---

[1] The words are for the most part Luke's words : τῇ αὐτῇ ἡμέρᾳ (cp. e.g. ἐν δὲ ταῖς ἡμέραις ταύταις, in the same position, Acts vi. 1). Θεασάμενος (Gospel, v. 27; Acts xxi. 27, etc.). Τινα ἐργαζόμενον (Gospel, xiii. 14). Τῷ σαββάτῳ (xiii. 14). Εἶπεν αὐτῷ Ἄνθρωπε (these three words as in xii. 14; cf. v. 20; xxii. 58, 60; ἄνθρωπε is nowhere found beside in Luke, Paul, and James ii. 20). Εἰ μὲν (Acts xviii. 14; xix. 38; xxv. 11; never in Matthew, Mark, John). Οἶδας τί ποιεῖς (Gospel, xxiii. 34). Μακάριος εἰ (Gospel, xiv. 14, etc.). Εἰ δὲ μὴ οἶδας, ἐπικατάρατος (only in Paul, Galatians iii. 10, 13, and perhaps John vii. 49). Καὶ παραβάτης (only in Paul and James). Παραβ. τοῦ νόμου (Romans ii. 25, 27; James ii. 11). There is, however, one difficulty, viz., that we should expect εἰ δὲ οὐκ οἶδας in New Testament Greek, or else εἰ δὲ μὴ (γε) without verb, cf. x. 6; xiii. 9.

the Romans strike out the verse in their copies? Because they found it was absent from the Oriental MSS., which must have appeared to them, as early as in the second century, more trustworthy than their own, or at least sufficient to render dubious the authority of anything which did not exist in them; and of course the Roman Church, at that time as in later times, cared much for being reputed thoroughly orthodox and untainted by untrustworthy doctrines or writings.

Neither are we quite devoid of instances of additions which are much akin to this; but here I shall speak only of one addition, which is, it is true, not preserved in D, nor in any Latin versions, but only in some Greek minuscule MSS. derived from a common original, which probably was very ancient, and existed somewhere in Southern Italy or Sicily. These MSS. have been carefully studied by my learned and much esteemed friend Professor Rendel Harris; they are commonly called the Ferrariani, because the affinity of some of them was first observed by a Dublin professor, the late W. H. Ferrar. The passage in question is a very long one, and extremely well known, only not as a part of Luke's Gospel, but as a part of John. I am speaking of the section about the adulteress, John vii. 53–viii. 11, which is now generally recognized not to have

belonged originally to John's Gospel. The reasons
for this decision you may find in Westcott and Hort:
that it does not exist in the whole mass of ancient
and trustworthy Greek Oriental MSS., including the
metrical paraphrase of the Gospel made by Nonnus;
that it is wholly unknown to all the Greek fathers,
down to the time of Chrysostom and Cyril, nay,
down to the tenth or even twelfth century; that it
is not unanimously assigned to this particular place
in John, but is placed by some witnesses at the close
of this Gospel, by others after vii. 36 or vii. 44;[1]
lastly, that it neither has the well-known and very
definite style of John, nor does it suit the tenor of
the narrative into which it has been thrown. But
as there are two places assigned to it in documental
tradition, one in John, and another, as I have said, in
Luke, it by no means follows that it is altogether
spurious, if it is proved not to belong to one of
these places. I may state at once that, according to
Eusebius (*Hist. Eccl.* 3. 39, 17), either this or a
similar story was told by Papias, and found in the
Gospel according to the Hebrews (καθ᾽ Ἑβραίους),
and that it has been conjectured that it came into
John from there; but it is only just to examine first
its claim to a place in Luke's Gospel, and in the case
of this also being proved unfounded, then to refer it

[1] *See* Nestle, *Einführung in das Gr. N.T.*, p. 102.

back to an apocryphal source. Now, which place in
Luke's Gospel is claimed by it? The place is in
chap. xxi., after the great sermon on the destruction
of the temple and the end of the world; in the
Ferrariani it follows the last verse of that chapter,
and the connection is this: (ver. 38) "And all the
people came early in the morning to Him in the
temple, for to hear Him. (=John vii. 53) And every
man went into his own house. (=viii. 1 f.) Jesus
went unto the Mount of Olives. And early in the
morning He came into the temple, and all the people
came unto Him," etc. Impossible, you will say; and
very justly. My young friend, E. Lippelt, who was
the first to call my attention to the Lucan character
of this section, and to this chapter as a fit place for
it, did not regard it as wholly impossible; but nevertheless I feel compelled to make two changes against
the authority of the Ferrariani: in the first place
wholly to cancel the introductory words, "And every
man went unto his own house," which are absent
from the Latin Corbeiensis (f^2), and are, in my opinion
nothing but the link of connection added to the section
in order to adjust it to the place in John, and secondly
to place it two verses earlier. Now, the connection
becomes the following: "And (after the great sermon)
Jesus went unto the Mount of Olives. And early in
the morning He came again into the temple, and all

the people came unto Him," etc. (the rest of the
section, ending with Jesus' words to the woman).
"And (Luke xxi. 37 f.) in the day time He was
teaching (ʾΗν δὲ τὰς ἡμέρας διδάσκων, imperfect of
custom) in the temple; and at night He went out, and
abode (ἐξερχόμενος ηὐλίζετο, imperf.) in the mount
that is called the Mount of Olives. And all the people
came early in the morning (ὤρθριζεν, imperf.) for to
hear Him." I venture to say that this connection is
so perfect that it cannot be the result of chance, but
must really go back to the author. There is first an
account of what came to pass on the next day, and
after that a general summary of what came to pass on
all of these days, given partly in the same words as
the beginning of the special account, but a little more
circumstantially, since a general custom deserved more
words than the occurrence of a single day. There is
an account somewhat akin to this in the β text of the
Acts, xv. 41—xvi. 4: "And he went through Syria
and Cilicia, confirming the brethren, and delivering the
decrees of the apostles and elders. After having gone
through these nations, he came to Derbe and to Lystra
(in Lycaonia)." Then (xviii. 1-3) about Timothy; and,
in conclusion (v. 4): "And going through the cities,
they preached unto them with all confidence the Lord
Jesus Christ, delivering at the same time the decrees
of the apostles and elders who were in Jerusalem."

Since, then, the place in Luke's Gospel claimed by the section in question (according to the Ferrariani) really seems to have been its original place, the second question will be, whether its style may be pronounced to be Luke's or not. Now, we may safely pronounce it so; but I prefer not to give here the discussion in detail, having already given it elsewhere,[1] and the case being that everybody, who is in possession of a concordance, may inquire into the matter for himself. That in this long passage, which is besides of a peculiar kind, there are some words not occurring elsewhere in Luke, is in accordance with what we find in any other piece of Luke's writing (*see* above on p. 113 f. 118).

To sum up, there is external evidence for the section's place having been in Luke's xxi.,[2] it really fits perfectly well into that place, and its style is quite that which is to be expected in the case of Lucan origin. Is this all we may demand? No; for everybody will ask: How, then, was it possible that the section lost almost completely its original place? and how did it pass from Luke into John? Unless we see at least the possibility of these things, we cannot restore it to its place in Luke. Has there

---

[1] *See* my edition of Luke on p. xlviii.

[2] There is besides the evidence of a Greek evangelistary (nr. 435), which gives this section as a part of Luke (ἐκ τοῦ κατὰ Λ.).

perhaps been offence taken at it by some very ancient
and highly authoritative Christian teachers? But
although offence might be taken, this result, viz., that
this long piece was omitted from all the ancient
Oriental MSS., nay, as regards Luke, from almost all
MSS., and that it was unknown to all the ancient
fathers of the Greek Church, nay as a part of Luke, to
all the fathers of the Greek and Latin Church—never
can be explained in this way. There is but one
solution possible: the section must give up all claim
to the Oriental form of Luke, and content itself
with claiming a place only in the Roman Luke.
Under this supposition a large part of the difficulties above stated vanish at once, and the rest cease
to be insurmountable. Suppose that early in the
second century the Roman Church found that it
had in its Gospel a very remarkable narrative, which
was disclaimed by all Eastern copies and authorities.
To allege that this form of the Gospel had been given
to the Roman Church by St. Luke himself, at a time
anterior to the Neronian persecution, by which the then
existing community of Christians had been almost
entirely destroyed, would be not so very easy, those
ancient facts being no longer upon record. On the
other hand, the charge of having an unauthenticated
Gospel must be avoided at any price. So the Church
of Rome, not finding in itself that strength of resistance

which it possessed at a later time, banished from its copies of Luke's Gospel all the seemingly unwarranted parts, and for that reason the section in question is not known, as far as we can see, to any Latin father before the fourth century. Perhaps even Marcion ignored it, although the fact of its not existing in Marcion's Gospel does not go far enough to prove that: he might have his individual reasons for omitting this section. as well as a great many other passages. Nevertheless, the section did not wholly perish, but was permitted to exist in some copies as a kind of appendix to Luke's Gospel, or (as now in Westcott and Hort's edition) to the Gospels in general; even the record of its original place must have been preserved somewhere, by some adscript, for instance, made to the end of the twenty-first chapter: *Here comes in the passage on the adulteress.* For if there existed in an archetype of the Ferrariani a remark of this tenor, a copyist might be induced to take out the section from St. John and put it in here in such a way, that it is not quite at the right place, and yet does not drop the additional link to John which it had received at its beginning. So far we do not find any serious difficulty; but the other question still remains unanswered: How did it come into John? It existed there, though only in the West, as early as in the fourth century, as we gather from the attestations

by Ambrose, Augustine, Jerome; we even see that it
was held in much esteem, and that its omission in a
part of the copies was ascribed to the supposition
of some jealous husbands having struck it out. Nor
did Jerome venture to banish it from his corrected
Latin version, which he certainly ought to have
done on his principle of going by the standard
of the Oriental Greek copies. So, having got a very
strong hold on its new seat in John, it finally gained
the East too, and is nowadays even better known
than a great many other stories in the New Testament.
But it remains quite unknown and undecided, who
brought the section into this place in John; even
the reasons for such an act can be but imperfectly
guessed.   If it formed, at some time in the third
century, a kind of appendix to the Gospels, and
seemed to some authoritative person in the West,
whoever he was, to be both authentic and of a special
value, he would seek out for it a fit place in one of the
four Gospels, and might imagine that Christ's not
judging the woman stood in a close relation to John
viii. 15, where He says: " Ye judge after the flesh;
I judge no man," wherefore he put in the section at
the next fitting place before that verse.   And so
we may leave this interesting question, stating so
much, that as long as the chain of external and
internal evidence remains unbroken, by which it is

proved that the section about the adulteress is both Lucan and absent from the Oriental Luke, we have in it the firm proof for the existence of a different early Roman Luke, that is, for the existence of two authentic forms of Luke.

There is still one question which may be asked: Has Luke intentionally left out this piece in a? or did it come to him from some fresh source, after he had written a? If I am to pronounce on such a question, I should regard the second alternative as rather improbable, and should prefer the first, there evidently being the same reasons for leaving out this section as for not giving the verse, vi. 5. Christian Jews might have taken offence at this position of Jesus regarding the Mosaic law, which might seem to be practically abolished by Him. We must bear in mind, that the woman's being stoned, according to the law, was actually out of the question; by answering in the affirmative, Jesus would have given the Jews an opportunity for denouncing Him to the Roman authority, which had deprived the Jews of the right of putting anybody to death (*see* John xviii. 31). But whoever did not bear that in mind, and was, although a Christian, still zealous for the law (*see* Acts xxi. 20), might be offended, and Luke did not care to give unnecessary offence by publishing this narrative in a country where there

were many thousands of Christians of that description
(Acts *l.c.*). In Rome, on the other hand, he might
feel himself quite at liberty and not bound to any
reticence.

CHAPTER X.

SOME OTHER TEXTUAL DIFFICULTIES IN LUKE'S GOSPEL.

I SHALL not give other proofs for the double form of Luke's Gospel; but nevertheless we cannot leave this Gospel yet, since there are many other passages in it of high importance, of which some elucidation may be given from textual criticism. We shall follow the order of the book itself.

In ii. 7 there is a reading attested by Epiphanius in his book against heresies (51. 9 ; ii. 460 f., Ddf.). Luke relates, says he, that the Child had been wrapped in swaddling clothes, and lay in a manger and in a cave (ἐν φάτνῃ καὶ [ἐν] σπηλαίῳ), because there was no room in the inn. Now this cave is even now generally known, not from Luke or any other part of Holy Scripture, but from tradition ; there is nowadays existing in Bethlehem the cave and a splendid basilica, which has been

built over it. The tradition is attested as early
as Origen (against Celsus, 1. 51), and Justin (Dialogue
with Tryphon, lxxviii.), unless the latter is directly
quoting from Luke; his words are: "Since Joseph
had not in that village a house where he might
lodge, he found accommodation in a certain cave
belonging to the village." I hesitate to reject this
evidence, especially that given by Epiphanius, and
do believe that there were copies of Luke containing
that reading. It differs from the ordinary one in
two points more, viz., that Epiphanius gives "He lay,"
where the corresponding word in the common Greek
text is not "laid" ($\check{\epsilon}\theta\eta\kappa\epsilon$), but "laid Him down" ($\dot{a}\nu\acute{\epsilon}$-
$\kappa\lambda\iota\nu\epsilon\nu$), and that in the next clause he omits "to them"
($a\dot{\nu}\tau o\hat{\iota}s$). Now these two readings are likewise found
in Latin witnesses and partly in Justin, and so we
may easily be induced to ascribe the whole of Epiphanius' reading to the form β, although it cannot
be shown in what way the writer came by that
form, or by this part of it, whether directly or indirectly; for it may well be that he is borrowing from
another writer. At any rate, this form of the passage is quite in harmony with itself, and may seem
preferable to the ordinary one. It could not be said,
"they laid Him *down* in a manger and in a cave," but
"laid (the general and indefinite word) Him in a manger and in a cave" might be said; moreover, to "inn,"

or generally, a "place where one could find lodgings" (for the Greek word κατάλυμα by no means excludes private accommodation), the cave gives a much better contrast than the manger, which (if the cave is left out) may be supposed to have belonged to the inn or to the private house. I scarcely need to mention the well-known fact, that caves were and are much used in the Orient for stalls, in which case they must of course contain a manger. So I should say that Luke's archetype is rendered here by β and not by α, and that possibly the preference given to the more expressive word "to lean" (ἀνακλίνειν) had induced the author to leave out the cave in α. Instead of "she wrapped up" and "she laid," there is in the Latin codex e the very commendable reading, "they wrapped . . . they laid"; the other one may be a mere corruption occasioned by the preceding, "she brought forth" (ἔτεκεν). Neither Epiphanius nor Justin tells against this correction.

We proceed to the third chapter, where the baptism of Christ is told, and in connection with it His genealogy is given. Whence this connection? Would not the proper place for the genealogy be either in the first or in the second chapter? Editors are accustomed to begin a fresh paragraph with the genealogy, or to leave a blank space, signifying that

they find here a break and not a connection. But
if we want to understand this strange sequel, we
have only to look into D. Not that here again
a difference of the two forms is to be recognized;
I am very far from pretending this solution to be
as it were a key which unlocks all doors. On the
contrary, there are very many cases where the reading
of D is a mere corruption, and other cases where
the reading of the a-witnesses is nothing but corrupt.
Now, if there are manifold other causes and kinds
of alteration, the one which most predominates in
the Gospels is their being jumbled with each other.
We must therefore be on our guard, whenever one
of two contending readings is at the same time universally attested in another Gospel or other Gospels,
that we may not be deceived by the authority of
MSS. which are by no means exempt from conflation.
In the passage in question (iii. 22), the words from
heaven are according to the great bulk of MSS.:
" Thou art my beloved Son; in Thee I am well
pleased." But, according to D and some Latin
witnesses (this evidence being supported by Justin
and by other fathers), the words are, " Thou art
my Son, to-day have I begotten Thee." If we
look into Matthew and Mark, we find in Matthew
(iii. 17) very nearly, and in Mark (i. 11) exactly
the same reading as in the common text of Luke.

This must render us suspicious, and make us attend very carefully to other individualities of Luke's passage, in order to see which of the two readings is in accordance with those. Now, the words following in Luke are these: "And Jesus Himself began to be about thirty years of age, being, as was supposed, the son of Joseph, which was the son of Heli," and so on. We have seen already that there is no connection between this sequel and the preceding words as they are commonly read; but there is a very clear connection if we take the words given by D. The " *to-day* have I begotten Thee" stands in opposition to the thirty years, and the "Thou art *my* Son," likewise to "being as was supposed the son of *Joseph.*" This therefore is the genuine reading, and the other one a product of assimilation to the other Gospels; for I cannot believe that there was ever a *material* discrepancy between the two authentic forms, as there would be in this case if we chose to regard one reading as that of a and the other as that of β. The words in the following verse offer many and very great additional difficulties which I cannot expound here; I will only point out that the "began to be" (23), $\dot{a}\rho\chi\acute{o}\mu\epsilon\nu o\varsigma$, appears to be a corruption from $\dot{\epsilon}\rho\chi\acute{o}\mu\epsilon\nu o\varsigma$, "when He came" *scil.* to the baptism ($\dot{\epsilon}\rho\chi\acute{o}\mu\epsilon\nu o\varsigma$ is given by the minuscule codex 700, *see* above on p. 61; $\dot{\epsilon}\rho\chi\acute{o}\mu\epsilon\nu o\varsigma$

ἐπὶ τὸ βάπτισμα, by Clement of Alexandria, and together with the corruption ἀρχόμενος by Irenaeus), and that the rest of the verse must, in my opinion, be restored in this way, that the qualifying clause, "as was supposed," refers both to the thirty years and to the fatherhood of Joseph.[1] Certainly a disciple of Paul could not ignore the eternal pre-existence of Christ, and the passage of the Psalm (ii. 7), which is likewise referred to Christ by Paul in the speech related in Acts xiii. 33, and by the author of the Epistle to the Hebrews (i. 5 ; v. 5), might be interpreted not of a definite day, but of the whole of eternity. But as these are purely theological questions, I shall not venture to enter in them further.

As for the genealogy immediately following, the difficulties with reference to that in Matthew are enormously great, and far surpass my ability to solve them. It seems to me an unwarranted supposition that the genealogy given by Luke is that of Mary and not of Joseph, although, by the way, the Davidic descent of Mary is also attested by the Western reading in ii. 4, 5, which runs thus : " And Joseph also went up unto the city of David, which is called Bethlehem, to

---

[1] The text finally adopted by me is this : ἦν δὲ Ἰησοῦς [ἐρχόμενος] ὡς ἐτῶν τριάκοντα, ὡς ἐνομίζετο, υἱὸς Ἰωσὴφ κ.τ.λ., "Jesus was, when He came (to the baptism), about thirty years old, as was supposed, and the son of Joseph," etc.

be taxed with Mary his wife,[1] because *they were* of the house and lineage of David." This reading gives also a good reason for Mary's accompanying Joseph on this journey, instead of remaining in Nazareth, which would otherwise have been more convenient to her condition. But as Luke expressly says, "the son of Joseph, who was the son" etc., it is clear that at least according to his own opinion, he did not give here the forefathers of Mary. What I have to discuss in this place is the very remarkable fact that, if we are to credit D, the discrepancy between Matthew and Luke is altogether non-existent, because D (but D alone in this case) gives the same names of the forefathers as Matthew does. The order of course is the inverse, being the ascending, as we call it, while Matthew has the descending order. But is not this a clear case of assimilation of one Gospel to another? After having decided the critical question we were treating just now, by giving the preference to the non-assimilated reading, we are bound to abide by the same principle, the more so as cases of assimilation are even more frequent in D than in other MSS., and as D stands

---

[1] "The espoused wife" of the ordinary text is a very clear corruption, due to an assimilation to i. 27 (where the case is quite different), and to dogmatic prejudices like those which have influenced the text of Matthew (*see* above on p. 86). At the time of chap. ii. Joseph had already "taken his wife unto him" (Matt. i. 24).

quite unsupported. It is true that there is a special reason which may be alleged in favour of D, viz., that the list of names is not quite identical with that in Matthew. The latter is incomplete, the number of names after David until the carrying away to Babylon having been reduced to thirteen, by the omission of four kings; now D in Luke has these four kings, and the supposition may be made, that Luke himself has given in his later edition this full list, which he found not in Matthew but in Matthew's authority, and which seemed to him more trustworthy than his own formerly given.[1] But if Luke used the same author as Matthew, and had access to the full list, he ought to give more names in another part too, which must be deemed to be even more incomplete than that from David to the Babylonian captivity. Matthew divides his list into three parts, each of fourteen names as he expressly states (ver. 17); the second part, that from David downwards, contains now but thirteen, very likely because of the omission of one name (that of Joiakim or Eliakim) in the MSS.[2]

[1] A similar supposition *has* been made by Ferd. Graefe (*see* above on p. 140) in *Theolog. Studien und Kritiken*, 1898, 123 ff. He relies especially on the different spelling of the names in D and in Matthew, *e.g. Abia* M., *Abiud* D in Luke. But Semitic names and words in the New Testament are hardly ever without variations, and what is to be compared with D of Luke is the Western Matthew (D itself wanting in this part). Now the Western Matthew (*c, k,* etc.) gives *Abiuth, Abiud,* or *Abiu.*

[2] *See* Graefe, p. 124.

That part comprehends a space of about four hundred years, and ought to contain, as we have seen, seventeen names; the three others must have been left out by Matthew himself. Now the third part (which in Luke comes first), comprehending about six hundred years, ought to have about twenty-six names, and yet it has but fourteen in D of Luke as in Matthew. We are bound to conclude therefore that the four names come from the Book of Kings, and their insertion may be due to any reader acquainted with that book; there are even in Matthew various readings giving this supplement. In this case therefore the evidence of D must be rejected; but there is still another one in the same genealogy which is of a different nature. The common text of Luke has between Sala and Arphaxad (ver. 35 f.) one Cainan, in accordance with the Greek Old Testament, but at variance with the Hebrew, where this personage is altogether wanting. Now D omits this Cainan. Is this a correction made by means of the Hebrew text? That seems to be very unlikely, since the readers of Luke, with a very few exceptions (as Jerome), were unacquainted with Hebrew. But the insertion of Cainan into the common text may have been made by means of the Greek Old Testament, just as in the case of the four kings. So here we shall conversely adopt the text of D, as in ver. 22, but as we there did without any reference to the special Roman form.

In the beginning of the eleventh chapter, where the prayer of our Lord is given, there are again very serious variations in the reading, both in the introduction to the prayer and in the prayer itself. The introduction as far as regards the disciples' words: "Lord, teach us to pray, as John also taught his disciples," is the same everywhere. But in the following words of our Lord D gives this amplified text: "When ye pray, use not vain repetitions as the rest do ; for some think that they shall be heard for their much speaking." Why, this is again Matthew, you will say at once. Only that Matthew has not "the rest," but "the heathen,"[1] nor "some think," but "they think." The expression, "as the rest do" (ὡς οἱ λοιποί), is besides well in accordance with Luke ; we may compare xviii. 11, "I thank Thee that I am not as the rest of men" (ὡς οἱ λοιποὶ τῶν ἀνθρώπων), while there is not any close parallel to it in the other Gospels (John never uses λοιπός). It is even more important that both the general tenor of this introduction, and in particular the words "as the rest do," are extremely well suited to all that precedes or follows. Shortness is recommended ; now, our Lord's prayer, according to Luke, is even shorter than accord-

[1] The Vatic. B gives not ἐθνικοί but ὑποκριταί, by assimilation to the preceding verses (2, 5).

ing to Matthew. It is John the Baptist whose example is alleged by the disciple; John, then, and his disciples must be included by the expression, "the rest," and the fact of John's disciples making no fewer prayers than the Pharisees is attested by Luke, and by Luke alone (v. 33): "Why do the disciples of John fast often, and make prayers, and likewise the disciples of the Pharisees; but Thine eat and drink?" where the addition "and make prayers" is absent from Mark and Matthew. I do not think that a reading may be safely discarded as worthless, when there is so much to be said in favour of it. But if it does not come from Matthew, whence does it come? All the words, with these few exceptions, are the same as in Matthew. How shall we explain that? Of course by the assumption, that Luke and Matthew had some Greek source in common; that assumption must, in my opinion, be made at any rate, because verbal agreement between Luke and Matthew, if rare upon the whole, exists nevertheless in some measure, and because that Luke borrowed from Matthew is excluded by cogent reasons, since he did not know any Gospel bearing the name of an apostle (*see* above on p. 16). But Matthew may have borrowed from Luke. If you apply this to the passage in question, you have already granted that D's reading is genuine Luke, and even if you except this one case, you are sustaining a thesis

which you will find very hard to prove.[1] Well, you
will say, I grant the common source, but how is it to
be explained that D alone has the words ? For there
is really no other witness for them but D, as in the
case of vi. 5, or in that of the genealogy. Since it
would be untenable to assume an omission in the
common text, nothing remains but to recognize here a
difference between the two forms. But β is the
shorter one, not α. True, if you except some cases where
Luke left out in α what might give offence to Oriental
readers. But this is not the case here. On the
contrary, might there not be Oriental readers still
adhering to John the Baptist ? In Rome there was
of course no one of that kind ; but for Palestine the
persistence of John's sect is well attested, and Luke,
when writing for those countries, might have his
reasons for considering the feelings of that sect.

But there is indeed a strange mixture of good and
bad in this codex Bezae (as there is, by the way, in
every "good" and ancient manuscript). Here it
alone has preserved something valuable, and in the
next verses it is in agreement with the mass of
untrustworthy witnesses, which exhibit the Lord's

---

[1] The thesis has been sustained (in a very clever way) by G.
Schläger in *Theol. Studien und Krit.*, 1896, 83 ff. See also my edition
of Luke's Gospel, xix. f. Schläger, too, does not *always* attend to
various readings. Matt. xxii. 35, νομικὸς is an interpolation coming
from Luke.

Prayer not in the shorter form of genuine Luke, but in the enlarged one of Matthew. I need not dwell on a question decided long ago. Our best witnesses give the prayer in Luke in this form: "Father, hallowed be Thy name. Thy kingdom come. Give us day by day our daily bread. And forgive us our sins, for we also forgive everyone that is indebted to us. And lead us not into temptation." Or, is not even this genuine Luke? That it is not is asserted by no less a personage than the well-known Gregory of Nyssa, who expressly states that Luke has instead of "Thy kingdom come," "Thy Holy Ghost come upon us and make us clean." Nor does he stand alone and unsupported: there is, in the first place, another ecclesiastic writer, Maximus Confessor, attesting the same; secondly, at least one of our own MSS., the minuscule codex 700 (*see* above on p. 61 and 169), actually has this reading;[1] thirdly, there is Marcion, in whose Gospel, according to Tertullian, these words stood side by side with "Thy kingdom come," the first part of the prayer, "Hallowed be Thy name," having been suppressed. Lastly, D itself has preserved the two words, "upon us" (ἐφ' ἡμᾶς), which stand in D before ἐλθέτω. As this appears to be the result of a conflation (*see* Professor Sanday in Westcott-Hort) so also is Marcion's text; in the copy used by

---

[1] Ἐλθέτω τὸ πνεῦμά σου τὸ ἅγιον ἐφ' ἡμᾶς καὶ καθαρισάτω ἡμᾶς.

him the original Lucan words, "Hallowed be Thy name," had given way to the adscript coming from Matthew, "Thy kingdom come." For it is not likely in any way that there were in Luke's original form two adjacent clauses beginning with the same word ἐλθέτω. I believe therefore that Gregory and codex 700 give the true Lucan text, and that Luke's form of the prayer differed even more from Matthew's than is commonly thought, of course as well in the Oriental copy as in the Roman, so important a difference between the two being wholly incredible. But which form, or which author, is more deserving of our trust? Luke or Matthew? Theologians perhaps will not hesitate to give an answer; but I deny the right of putting the alternative, until another question is settled. Are both of our authors speaking of the same thing? Certainly, it will be answered, for the introduction is the same in both, if D's reading there is to be considered genuine. Matthew cut off the question asked by the disciple in order to insert the prayer into the great sermon. I was indeed just now supposing a Greek authority common to Matthew and Luke, and it may be argued that Luke has preserved the true form given by that authority. And Matthew, I shall answer, has combined and welded that authority with another authority, or else Luke has done the same. What means are there to decide such questions? As long as scholars dream of one definite primitive Gospel, in open contradiction to Luke's proem, they will both raise and answer them; but as soon as that unwarranted supposition is removed we get rid of a host of inextricable questions.   As for the *welded* character of either account, it is to be noticed that the words of the prayer in Luke and Matthew, even when there is a substantial agreement between them, are but partly the same, and that more comes into the question than abridgment or enlargement.

In the account of the Supper of our Lord (xxii. 7 ff.) the divergencies between the different witnesses for Luke's text are uncommonly great, and its ordinary form is indeed far from satisfactory.   I have proposed elsewhere [1] a very radical solution, striking out not only vers. 19*b* and 20, but also ver. 19*a*, and by these means establishing a narrative both clear and consistent in itself, but not containing any longer the institution of the Lord's Supper.   Now, I hardly need say, that I have not been determined by any theological reasons.   The audacity and presumption of theologians—I speak chiefly of some German theologians—is nowhere exhibited more scandalously than here: they mount by the sole force of their

---

[1] See *Theolog. Studien und Kritiken*, 1896, p. 733 ff.   The subject has been very carefully expounded in that same journal by F. Graefe, 1896, p. 250 ff. ; 1898, p. 134 ff.

genius higher than St. Paul, into the very mind of
our Lord, and bring back revelations according to
which the Christian Church, nay even its founders,
the apostles, have been strangely deceived about
the real sense of this institution, or about its being
an institution at all. As for myself, I have no desire
to mount their Pegasus, who will very soon throw
his rider, a new Bellerophon, and am content to walk
on earth and to scrutinize the evidence of MSS., not in
order to get a sublime recognition of " spiritual things,"
which are far above the reach of the "natural
man" (1 Cor. ii. 14), that is both of philology and
of scientific theology, but to find out, if possible, what
Luke or another of our authorities has really written.
Now the vers. 19b and 20, which closely agree with
Paul (1 Cor. xi. 24 f.), are left out by D and other
witnesses; ver. 19a, which agrees with Mark, is not
left out by any witness; but its position not being the
same in all the witnesses, that verse too becomes
suspicious.   Moreover, we must find a reason for the
whole mass of variations, that is to say an original
text, which invited, as it were, readers to alterations
and additions; at the same time the required text
must be irreproachable from another point of view,
which we may suppose to have been that of the
author.   The text of Westcott and Hort, who leave
out vers. 19b, 20, but retain 19a, does not answer to

the latter condition, since the institution of the cup
is wholly wanting; Luke is not to be supposed to
have given a mutilated account, but either no account
at all, or a complete one. The latter alternative
being apparently excluded, if we are to explain the
variants—for the complete, and at the same time,
orderly text would not have given any offence—there
is but the former remaining, that is the supposition
that Luke chose to leave out what was commonly
known to his readers. As a matter of fact, this
point is not his only omission, since he does not
relate anywhere how the betrayer was disclosed by
Jesus, nor is he the only evangelist who omits the
institution of the Lord's Supper, since the case is the
same in John. But later readers did not understand
his intention, and either inserted both bread and cup
from St. Paul (vers. 19*b*, 20), or, wrongly imagining
that the cup was already there (in ver. 17 f.), they
inserted the bread from Mark. I entreat my readers
to read the narrative for themselves, leaving out ver.
19 f., and to ask themselves if this form is not quite
satisfactory under the single supposition, that it was
not Luke's intention to relate the institution of the
Lord's Supper. The sequence, " For I say unto you,"
etc. (ver. 18), and "But ($\pi\lambda\dot{\eta}\nu$) behold, the hand of
him that betrayeth me," etc. (ver. 21), is much like
that in xviii. 8: " I tell you that . . . Nevertheless

($\pi\lambda\dot{\eta}\nu$) when the Son of Man," etc., or in xix. 26 f.:
"For I say unto you, that . . . But ($\pi\lambda\dot{\eta}\nu$) those mine
enemies," etc. Leaving the matter to the reader's
consideration, I add only this, that the insertion from
Paul must have been made in the very oldest times
by some man who possessed Paul's writings, but did
not possess either Matthew or Mark; it is self-evident
that there actually was a time when many persons
and Christian communities were in that condition.

There is an expanded text in D and other witnesses
(among which for once Origen comes in) in ver. 24 ff.
of the same chapter; as there is no material difference,
I recognize here the original form of the Roman text.
The same text has something more on the healing of
the servant whose ear had been cut off by Peter (ver.
51). Then, in ver. 53 D gives a very remarkable
reading, by which the text is considerably improved.
Instead of: "But this is your hour and the power of
darkness" ($\tau o \hat{v} \ \sigma \kappa \acute{o} \tau o v s$), D gives: "But this is your
hour and your power, darkness" ($\tau \grave{o} \ \sigma \kappa \acute{o} \tau o s$). The
words before these are: "When I was *daily* in the
temple, ye stretched forth no hands against me," and
it strikes one at once how much the text gains by
the clear and strong opposition coming out between
day and darkness. The ordinary reading must be due
to a copyist who had in mind Paul's words (Col. i. 13):
"Who hath delivered us from the power of darkness.'

In chap. xxiii. I notice first of all the apocryphal addition to ver. 5, which is given by two Latin witnesses: " And He alienates from us our sons and our wives; for they do not baptize (or ' wash ') themselves (cf. xi. 38), nor make themselves clean." Similarly Marcion's Gospel had in ver. 2: "We found this fellow perverting the nation, and *destroying the law and the prophets* (for these words there are Latin witnesses too; cf. Matt. v. 17), and forbidding to give tribute, and alienating the wives and the children, and saying," etc. The verses 10, 11, 12, are skipped in the Syriac palimpsest from Mount Sinai, and Professor Wellhausen[1] thinks this omission to be well-founded, since in ver. 15 Pilate says to the Jews: " Herod (for I sent Him [Jesus] to him) has not found," etc., telling them what they were evidently still ignorant of; so the statement in ver. 10 ("And the chief priests . . . accused Him," before Herod) is excluded. But that reading in ver. 15 is not the only one, nor is it, in my opinion, the right one; there is another: "for I sent you to him," and a third, which I prefer to the other two: "for he has sent Him back unto us." Was it possible, that Pilate, declining to be judge in this case, sent the accused to another tribunal, and did not send at the same time His accusers? The double text of Luke is out of question here; for D gives a special reading

[1] See *Göttinger Nachrichten*, 1895, p. 9.

for ver. 12, materially unimportant, but very remarkable because of the words.[1] So the omission of those verses by the Syriac witness must be considered accidental.

We pass on to ver. 44 f.: "And it was about the sixth hour, and there was a darkness over all the earth until the ninth hour. (45) And the sun was darkened, and the veil of the temple was rent in the midst." This again is one form of the text among many, and by no means an irreproachable one : why " and the sun was darkened" *after* "there was a darkness"? On the other hand, the Alexandrian reading in 45*a*, "the sun having been eclipsed" (ἐκλιπόντος), is open to the even more serious objection: How was it possible in the very midst of the lunar month, which was the time of the passover? I think this is an erroneous adscript (*see* Origen in Westcott-Hort), and go back to the wider attested reading (which is also, in the main, that of D), the case being that a very slight emendation, and an attested one, puts things right. Strike out the "and" before "the sun," according to the attestation of five Latin witnesses, and of D, which however has δὲ after ἐσκοτίσθη, and insert the same particle with one of these witnesses (the Vercellensis *a*) before " until,"

[1] Ὄντες δὲ ἐν ἀηδίᾳ ὁ Πιλᾶτος καὶ ὁ Ἡρῴδης ἐγένοντο φίλοι ἐν αὐτῇ τῇ ἡμέρᾳ. This is a very good instance of the occasional refinement of style found in β. Ἀηδία is new in Luke, but we have seen that he is constantly introducing words not again used by him.

and you have a text as good as need be: "there was a darkness over all the earth, and until the ninth hour the sun was darkened." The latter part of 45 is put by D alone after 46, which is the order of events given by Matthew and Mark.

A very interesting addition is made by D, together with the Latin *c* and the Sahidic version, to ver. 53 ; there begins besides with that verse a series of variants extending over the beginning of the next chapter. D's text in 53 is : "and laid it in a sepulchre . . . and after it had been laid there, he put unto the sepulchre a stone, which twenty men could scarce roll." Let me first say that the stone is there in Luke, as in the other Gospels, in the beginning of the next chapter (ver. 2); it must therefore seem strange that it was not mentioned before, as in Matthew and Mark.[1] In the text of D we miss nothing, neither can it be said that that text has received a supplement from another Gospel, since the words, and not only these, are quite peculiar. Even too peculiar, you will say. The addition in D has indeed, at first sight, a somewhat strange appearance ; my learned friend, Professor Rendel Harris, was reminded by it of a passage in Virgil,

---

[1] It is true that John too says nothing of the stone being put on the sepulchre, and nevertheless mentions it afterwards (*see* xix. 42 ; xx. 1).

and there lies even nearer at hand a similar one
in Homer, on the stone which the Cyclops put into
his door: "a stone which not even twenty-two carts
might carry away" (λίθον δ' ἐπέθηκε θύρηφιν ὄβριμον·
οὐκ ἂν τόν γε δύω καὶ εἴκοσ' ἄμαξαι ἐσθλαὶ τετράκυκλοι
ἀπ' οὔδεος ὀχλίσσειαν, *Odyss.* ix. 240). There we
have the twenty or twenty-two (carts in this case),
and we have the verb ἐπέθηκεν as in Luke β, while
Matthew and Mark use προσκυλίω. But let this
come from Homer; what is that against Luke's
authorship? Must we not accept it for a certainty
that Luke, the physician of Antioch, had gone through
his Homer? Nor are we devoid of other proofs for
this obvious fact: in Acts xxvii. 41, he says of
a sudden, ἐπέκειλαν τὴν ναῦν, although neither he nor
any other New Testament writer elsewhere employs
the obsolete word ἡ ναῦς, instead of which τὸ πλοῖον
was the common expression (occurring in this same
chapter no less than thirteen times), and ἐπι-
κέλλω, instead of ἐποκέλλω, is altogether poetical.
But in Homer, in that same book of the *Odyssey*,
he had read thus, νῆας . . . ἐπικέλσαι (148),
and again (546) νῆα ἐκέλσαμεν. But nevertheless
you will ask: Do you really mean to make Luke
embellish this narrative by a touch borrowed from a
heathen poet? I do not say that the touch is from
Homer, but that the stone seems to have reminded

him of that door-stone in Homer, and that therefore
the description is similar, but nevertheless neither
unreal nor exaggerated. As he had been in Jerusalem, he may be supposed to have gone and seen
the sacred places, and there the size of the stone
must have impressed him. Joseph, who was a rich
man, had as many workmen at his disposal as he
liked or thought necessary, and he chose a very
large stone in order that the sepulchre might not
be broken open and profaned by the hostile Jews.

Let us now see the continuation of the narrative in
D, ver. 54: "And that day was the preparation (or
'that of preparation'), and the Sabbath drew on." D
(the same thing in other and fewer words): "And it
was the day before the Sabbath" ($\pi\rho o\sigma a\beta\beta\acute{a}\tau o\upsilon$,
cf. Mark xv. 42). Ver. 55, instead of "the women,"
"two women," that is Mary Magdalene, and Mary the
mother of James and Joses, *see* Mark xv. 47 (Matt.
xxvii. 61). I think $\delta\acute{\upsilon}o$, "two," instead of $a\acute{\iota}$ is right,
since it is attested by Eusebius also; consequently in
xxiv. 1, the text of D, but also the common text (con-
tradicted it is true by the Vaticanus B, etc.) has an
enlargement of the subject: "and certain others with
them." This enlargement would be cancelled as
useless as soon as $\delta\acute{\upsilon}o$ had vanished from the text.
The end of 55 is again abridged in D, and in 56,
"according to the commandment" is left out by the

same MS. But in xxiv. 1 it has an enlarged form:
"Now upon the first day of the week, very early
in the morning, they went (ἤρχοντο, not ἦλθον, came)
unto the sepulchre, bringing *what* they had prepared with certain others with them. *And they
reasoned with themselves: Who shall roll away the
stone?*" "And *when they arrived* (ἐλθοῦσαι δὲ) they
found," etc. That addition comes from Mark xvi.
3, you will say. And yet Mark has not "reasoned,"
but "said" (ἔλεγον), nor τίς ἄρα, which is quite Lucan,
but simply τίς; and if "shall roll away the stone" is
in both, you must notice that the common form of
Luke has the same verb in the next verse. This, then,
is the special text of β, while in α, Luke, consistent
with himself, had omitted to mention the stone
as well here as in xxiii. 53.

I shall state, but *not* solve, one difficulty more.
Ver. 12 of the common text: "Then arose Peter,
and ran unto the sepulchre," etc., is left out by recent
editors on the evidence of D and its Latin associates,
with which, as Tischendorf thinks, Eusebius agrees.
Comparing John (xx. 3 ff.) we find an agreement
strongly arguing the interpolation of the verse in
Luke. The verse does not leave an apparent gap
at its place; on the contrary ver. 13, "two of them,"
joins with 11 and not at all with 12, which refers to
Peter and John exclusively. So far all is very well;

but when we come to ver. 24, we find there the same fact mentioned: "And certain of them which were with us went to the sepulchre," etc. Now, is this text, that of D, and of Westcott-Hort and Tischendorf, a consistent one? Why has not Luke given this important detail in its right place? Then, ver. 24 too is an interpolation; its removal does not leave a gap any more than 12. But neither have we evidence for that omission, nor is the verse found in John. As I have stated, I do not feel able to solve this difficulty; as an editor, I was bound to omit ver. 12 like Tischendorf and Westcott-Hort; but doubts still remain.

CHAPTER XI.

TEXTUAL CONDITION AND ORIGINAL SEPARATE
FORMS OF MARK'S GOSPEL.

AFTER having said so much on Luke, I shall be comparatively brief on the other two Gospels, that is on Mark and John, for we saw already that on Matthew, as regards the condition of his text, there is not much to be said. This is indeed not true either of Mark or of John; but with regard to them there is so much obscurity that I have not much to say about either.

To begin with the personality of Mark, it does not lie more in the shadow than that of Luke, but even less. His original name was John, and the Roman Mark a surname given in order to distinguish him (which was indeed much required) from other Johns; his mother was called Mary (as perhaps were one half of the women existing then in Judaea),[1] and possessed a

---

[1] In the Gospels we meet with five Marys, and besides them one Elizabeth, one Anne, one Joanna, one Susanna, and one Martha,

rather large house in Jerusalem (Acts xii. 12). It has been quite plausibly surmised that the young man having a linen cloth, who was in the company of Jesus on the night in Gethsemane, and who is mentioned by Mark alone (xiv. 51 f.), was nobody else but the author of that Gospel himself. He, as well as his mother, was a member of the early Church in Jerusalem, and afterwards accompanied Barnabas and Paul as an assistant on their first journey, but only as far as Pamphylia, from whence he returned to Jerusalem (Acts xiii. 5, 13). Barnabas supported him notwithstanding, but not Paul, for which reason, when they were to undertake their second journey, they separated (ibid. xv. 36 ff.).

Paul, in his Epistle to the Colossians (iv. 10), tells us that Mark was Barnabas' cousin; he himself had at length forgiven him, and had him at that time in his company, together with Luke (*see* also Philemon, ver. 24). Where that was, whether in Caesarea or in Rome, is a much discussed question. Again, Paul says in his Second Epistle to Timothy (iv. 11), which dates from his later captivity in Rome: "Only Luke is with me. Take Mark, and bring him with thee: for he is profitable to me for the *ministry*." But Mark seems to have been most of all with Peter, who calls him his son (1 Peter v. 13), and this agrees with the well-known words of Papias, who relates, on the authority of his "presbyter" (apparently John, *see* the next chapter), that Mark had been a follower and interpreter of Peter, and that this enabled him to write his Gospel (*see* above on p. 78). We are not warranted in giving to the word interpreter (ἑρμηνευτής) any other sense than it commonly has, that of one who translates the words spoken in one language into another, and in this case the one language must be Aramaic, and the other Greek. It is therefore to be supposed that Peter, when travelling in a country of mixed population, preached in Aramaic, and made Mark translate his words into Greek. That sojourn at Babylon and Peter's epistle fall into a late period; Papias' author may be supposed to speak chiefly of the very earliest period of Gospel-preaching, which was then confined to Judaea and the adjacent regions, down to the time when Peter, having escaped from Herod's prison, went into another place (Acts xii. 17).[1] After that time we find Mark in Barnabas' company, and then again in Jerusalem (whither Peter had meanwhile returned), and again, after Peter's departure to Antioch (and Babylon,

---

[1] I briefly state that ἑρμηνευτὴς γενόμενος means, "he *had* been" (before writing his Gospel), and nothing more. Whether the function of interpreter had come to a close by Peter's death (as Harnack asserts), or by Peter's going away into another country where an interpreter was not needed, is not stated.

see above, p. 26), he joins his cousin. Tradition
assigns to him the rôle of being the first preacher
in Egypt, and the first bishop of Alexandria (*see*
Eusebius, *Hist. Eccl.* ii. 14, 1), which see he is said
to have occupied until the eighth year of Nero,
that is 62 A.D. (ibid. ii. 24). It appears, therefore,
that apart from the apostles themselves perhaps
no man was better able to write a Gospel than
Mark, and that he was also a very fit personage
to write the history of the earliest Church in Jerusalem and Judaea. In a former chapter (*see* p. 141)
we hit upon the conjecture, that he actually did
write that history, and that Luke used his work for the
first part of his own Acts. So much is quite evident,
that for the story told in Acts xii. the authority
of Mark is claimed, as it were, by the narrator,
when he says (ver. 12): "He (Peter) came to
the house of Mary the mother of John, whose surname
was Mark"; and proceeds to say (ver. 17): "He
declared unto them (Mark is in all likelihood included) how the Lord had brought him out of the
prison." Now, I say that in case this conjecture
is right, Mark must have given the story of the
primitive Church in Aramaic, and not in Greek. For
Luke's authority was an Aramaic one, and if that
authority was a book by Mark, you see the consequence. But of course you will require proof

for the major premiss. I say, that the language
in the first twelve chapters of the Acts is markedly
different from that in the later chapters: in the
former Aramaicisms abound, in the latter they are
comparatively very scarce; from these facts I argue
that the second part is an independent work by
Luke, but the former depends on an Aramaic source.
I think I may dispense with giving the proofs here
in detail, as the Acts are not the proper subject
of the present little book, and as I have given
them elsewhere;[1] but at any rate, Professor Nestle's
discovery must be spoken of even here. There is
in the Acts (iii. 14) a passage where the ordinary
text runs thus: "But ye denied the Holy One,"
whilst D (together with Irenaeus) has instead of
" denied " (ἠρνήσασθε) the quite unintelligible reading
ἐβαρύνατε (something like "you troubled"). No
doubt "denied" is right, and ἐβαρύνατε utterly wrong;
but as the supposition of an ordinary corruption
is manifestly excluded, Professor Nestle is undoubtedly
right in supposing that Luke's Aramaic, or Hebrew
source, had here a word which might be easily
read and understood both ways, and that this word
was כפרתם, or (which is much alike in Semitic
writing) כברתם, the former meaning ἠρνήσασθε, and
the latter ἐβαρύνατε.[2]   There was a misunderstanding

---

[1] See my edition of Luke's Gospel, p. xxi ff.
[2] Theolog. Studien u. Kritiken, 1896, p. 102 ff.

of the Aramaic or Hebrew text, which crept into Luke's first text, but has been corrected in the second.

But here comes a rather serious objection in the shape of the question: Did Luke understand Aramaic? As for Hebrew, that is quite out of question; but his native town Antioch was situated in an Aramaic country. Nevertheless the town itself was of Greek origin, and it by no means follows that any Greek native of that town must understand the language spoken by the country-people around it, and perhaps by a part of the lower classes in the town itself. Even if he understood and spoke a little Aramaic, it does not follow that he could read Aramaic books. Well, then I say that Luke, having got Mark's book, which was written in Aramaic, got for himself an interpreter of it, and that the blunder *ἐβαρύνατε* is due to that interpreter, and the correction *ἠρνήσασθε* is due to a person better informed, perhaps to Mark himself, if he met with Luke either in Rome or elsewhere. It is even easier to explain the Aramaisms in Luke's first part, if he was using an authority translated from the Aramaic into bad Greek: copying from that authority, he corrected the Greek, but not so thoroughly as to abolish all traces of the Aramaic origin.

Let us now see what will follow from **the**

premisses we have hitherto stated. If Mark's second
part was written in Aramaic, then his first part,
that is the Gospel, must have been originally written
in the same language. Perhaps you will oppose
this by Papias, and Papias' authority, the presbyter.
Papias tells us, probably on the same authority,
that Matthew's Gospel was originally in Hebrew,
and that it had been translated or interpreted
(ἡρμήνευσε is again the word) differently according
to the different abilities of the interpreters (ὡς ἦν
δυνατὸς ἕκαστος). That is to say, Papias' presbyter
knew of different Greek forms of Matthew, besides
the Hebrew (or Aramaic) original, but in the case
of Mark, the interpreter of Peter, he knew only
one Greek form of that Gospel, and nothing at all
of an Aramaic original. Then, I say, he did not
know all that might be known, or even may be
known. Of course there is nothing remaining nowadays of an Aramaic Mark, but of the different
translations there are some traces still left in the
various readings given by our MSS. and other witnesses.

I shall take first a very clear case of triple
tradition. Mark xi. 13, in the story of the fig-tree
according to the Authorized Version, has: "He came,
if haply He might find anything thereon," which
renders this Greek text: ἦλθεν εἰ ἄρα τι εὑρήσει ἐν

αὐτῇ. But D (with the Latin *b*, *c*, etc.) exhibits the same text in very different words: ἦλθεν ἰδεῖν ἐάν τί ἐστιν ἐν αὐτῇ, "in order to see whether there was anything thereon"; and lastly, the valuable minuscule codex 700, in accord with a quotation in Origen and with three Latin witnesses, has at least a different construction: ἦλθεν ὡς εὑρήσων τι ἐν αὐτῇ, "thinking that He would find something thereon." I shall not allow you to decide this critical question upon authority of MSS., but demand an impartial hearing for the reasons which may be given in favour of each of the three readings. Material difference there is none, nor is there dependence on Matthew (*see* Matthew xxi. 19: ἦλθεν ἐπ' αὐτήν, nothing else); so we have only to examine the language. (A) ἦλθεν εἰ ἄρα. Why, this is Luke's style, *see* Acts vii. 1 (D); viii. 22; xvii. 27. In Mark there is no εἰ ἄρα besides this passage (although there is ἰδεῖν εἰ xv. 36), nor any ἄρα except in iv. 41, τίς ἄρα, and there too with an important variant. (B) ἦλθεν ἰδεῖν, see Mark v. 14, ἦλθον ἰδεῖν τί ἐστιν τὸ γεγονός. Ἐάν . . . ἐστιν is grossly incorrect, but not altogether unparalleled in New Testament Greek. (C) ὡς εὑρήσων: very good Attic, but hardly known to New Testament writers, with the exception of the Epistle to the Hebrews (xiii. 17). So we may give the preference to B, as

being most in accordance with Mark; but indeed
the whole of the case looks much like that described
by Papias: "everyone interpreted as he was able to
do" (ἡρμήνευσεν ὡς ἦν δυνατὸς ἕκαστος), in bad Greek
(B), or in better Greek (A), or in good Greek (C).
We may speak briefly of iv. 41, the passage we
were just now citing: instead of τίς ἄρα οὗτός ἐστιν,
ὅτι καὶ ὁ ἄνεμος καὶ ἡ θάλασσα αὐτῷ ὑπακούει, two Latin
witnesses simply give: ἴδε πῶς κ.τ.λ. ("the wind," etc.),
and this is the ordinary style of Mark, see ii. 24;
xiii. 1; xv. 4, while the other reading is Lucan.
But there is a difference here: not only is this
reading Lucan in character, but actually Lucan (see
Luke viii. 25) in the very same story; so the
decision will be that Mark's text here has suffered
by assimilation to the parallel passage in Luke, as
there are of course many cases of this character in
Mark as well as in other Gospels.

Again, in xv. 15, the ordinary text is: "And so
Pilate, willing to content the people, released Barabbas
unto them." But the words, βουλόμενος ποιῆσαι τὸ
ἱκανὸν τῷ ὄχλῳ or β. τῷ ὄχλῳ τὸ ἱκ. ποιῆσαι, are
omitted by D and two Latin versions, which have
nothing but ὁ δὲ Π. ἀπέλυσεν αὐτοῖς τὸν Βαραββᾶν.
There is here no assimilation, except in so far as
Matthew too gives the bare fact without any reason
for it; nevertheless you might try to explain the

omission as occasioned by Matthew, and argue that,
in D, the next words are evidently assimilated to
that Gospel: τὸν δὲ Ἰησοῦν φραγελλώσας παρέδωκεν,
etc., instead of καὶ παρ. (παρ. δὲ, B) τὸν Ἰησ. φραγ.
On the other hand, it is a well-known fact that
verbal agreement between these two Gospels exists
to a very large extent. Then, the curious thing is
that only here Mark uses βούλεσθαι instead of θέλειν
(which was the ordinary word for "to will," while
βούλεσθαι bears a somewhat learned character), and
that not even τὸ ἱκανὸν ποιεῖν occurs elsewhere in
the New Testament; nevertheless, when we turn to
Luke (who at least in the Acts makes a rather
large use of βούλεσθαι), we find there the similar
phrase τὸ ἱκανὸν λαβεῖν (Acts xvii. 9). So we may
recognize here again the forms A (in D) and B
(in the ordinary text), but in a different way, A
bearing an expanded character, and B an abridged one.

In ver. 19 of this chapter the same thing recurs:
"And they smote Him upon the head with a reed,
and did spit upon Him, and bowing their knees
worshipped Him." The Latin k (see above, p. 80 f.)
leaves out, "and did spit upon Him"; both D and
k leave out the last of the three clauses. So
Matthew, says Tischendorf. But the matter itself
is in Matthew, with a different word it is true, and
in a different place (γονυπετήσαντες, Matt. xxvii. 29,

in the place corresponding to Mark's ver. 18); why then, if there is in D assimilation to Matthew, do we not find in that MS. the corresponding addition? Moreover, the place of the clause in ver. 19 is altogether wrong, the worshipping belonging to the mockery told of in 18 and not to the cruelties in 19, and lastly, the phraseology is again Lucan: τιθέναι τὰ γόνατα is a phrase used by Luke alone, and by him five times, while Mark and Matthew say γονυπετεῖν (not occurring elsewhere in the New Testament), and Paul κάμπτειν τὰ γόνατα. Then the clause must be spurious in Mark. Very well, but it is not borrowed from Luke, although it bears his character.

There are more passages of the same kind: in ver. 24, where the soldiers are casting lots upon the garments of Christ, the words τίς τί ἄρῃ, which are good Greek and may find a parallel in Luke (xix. 15, AR, etc., Tischend.), are omitted by D and other Western witnesses, and a little before, in ver. 21, k offers a reading, agreeing closely with Mark's manner: ("they compel Simon,") *fuit autem nomen* (a gross blunder for *pater*) *Alexandri et Rufi, et faciunt eum crucem baiulare*; cf. vii. 25 f. ("a certain woman came,") ἦν δὲ ἡ γυνὴ (ἡ γυνὴ is omitted by b, etc.; the reading of BD, etc., is ἡ δὲ γυνὴ ἦν) Ἑλληνὶς . . ., καὶ ἠρώτα αὐτὸν κ.τ.λ. Then the whole ver. 28 : "And the scripture was fulfilled, which saith, And He was numbered with the transgressors," which is omitted by ℵ and B, and D and *k*, and many other good witnesses, is in accordance with Luke even more than with John : *see* for the Old Testament passage, Luke xxii. 37, and for the form of introduction, Acts i. 16 : "This scripture must needs have been (or 'be') fulfilled." You see that in this case the evidence against the apparently Lucan form is not confined to the West, and if you look further on, you find that the forms A (apparently Lucan) and B (apparently original Mark) are by no means connected in a definite way with definite witnesses.

In chapter xiv. 4 the common reading is : "And there were some that had indignation within themselves." The words and constructions used are quite in Mark's style. But D and Latin witnesses give the reading : οἱ δὲ μαθηταὶ αὐτοῦ διεπονοῦντο. This διαπονεῖσθαι (to feel pain or anger) is a very rare word, occurring but twice in the New Testament, namely in Acts iv. 2 ; xvi. 18. D's text therefore is here A and not B, and likewise in xiv. 25, οὐ μὴ προσθῶ πιεῖν, instead of (οὐκέτι) οὐ μὴ πίω. For this Hebraizing use of the verb προστιθέναι in the sense of " again " is similarly found in Luke xx. 11 f. ; Acts xii. 3 (where the middle voice

προστίθεσθαι is employed). Lastly, in xvi. 1, even
this distinction between A and B fails to suit the
facts, inasmuch as both readings there bear the
character of A. "And when the Sabbath was past"
(καὶ διαγενομένου τοῦ σαββάτου), a phrase exclusively
Lucan, *see* Acts xxv. 13; xxvii. 9. D has instead
of this and the following names of women nothing
but καὶ πορευθεῖσαι, the subject remaining the same
as before. But πορεύεσθαι too, although seemingly
a quite common verb, is never used in Mark,
except three times in the spurious close of his
Gospel (xvi. 10, 12, 15), while Luke employs it
like Matthew and John. It is, besides, evident
that the text of Mark in this place has suffered
seriously: "And Mary Magdalene and Mary the
mother of Joses beheld where He was laid (xv. 47).
And when the Sabbath was past, Mary Magdalene,
and Mary the mother of James, and Salome, had
bought sweet spices," etc. Is Mary the mother of
Joses a different person from Mary the mother
of James? By no means: a little before (xv. 40)
it was said: "And Mary the mother of James the
less and of Joses." A second difficulty: the "had
bought" of the English version is an attempt to
establish a harmony between Mark and Luke, who
tells us that they had bought the spices on Friday
evening (xxiii. 56); but the Greek text (ἠγόρασαν)

gives no warrant at all for this translation, and compels us to translate "they bought," which is indeed very strange, for then mention seems to be made of a neutral time between the end of the Sabbath (ver. 1) and the first day of the week (ver. 2). So the repeated catalogue of names in xvi. 1 seems spurious, and the "when the Sabbath was past" also. In fact, when these additions are removed, we have quite a clear narrative. But even if these additions are rejected, they must be at least explained, and how is that to be done?

To use a simile: reading Mark (with due attention given to the variants) reminds one of walking on quicksand, that is where the surface is quicksand while a little below there may be gravel or even rock; for the difference of readings mainly rests in the expressions, and does not affect the sense. But nevertheless we feel unsafe, and wonder in what way such a condition of the text may have been produced. It is true that the condition is nowhere else so bad as in this 16th chapter, where there is again in ver. 4 a wide difference between the witnesses, and the words "for it (the stone) was very great," which in the common text stand rather awkwardly, and which are besides again of a strongly Lucan character (*see* Luke xviii. 23, ἦν γὰρ πλούσιος σφόδρα; Mark never uses σφόδρα), are placed by D, and Eusebius, and others much more suitably at the end of the 3rd verse. The Latin *k*, in this respect, goes with the majority, but it has a long apocryphal addition in this place : " And suddenly, about the third hour (that is at nine o'clock), there was a darkness over all the earth, and angels descended from the heavens, and rising in the glory of the living God they mounted together with Him, and immediately there was light again. And the women approached the sepulchre," etc. As for the hour, we must notice that in *k* (and D, etc.), there is no " very " before " early " in ver. 2, and instead of " at the rising of the sun " (ἀνατέλλοντος τοῦ ἡλίου, or even ἔτι ἀνατ.) there is another well-attested reading, " after the rising (ἀνατείλαντος) of the sun." Here therefore the quick-sand seems to reach further below the surface. As we are speaking of *k*, it is worth noticing that this version at another place (xi. 4 ff.) exhibits a very strong contraction, giving nothing but : " And they went their way (4), and said even as Jesus had commanded them" (6), much in the same way as D in the corresponding place of Luke (*see* above on p. 149 f.).

You are looking, no doubt, for some clue which may show you the way out of this wilderness. It is of course impossible to hold the copyists responsible : we should have to charge them all alike with taking gross liberties, and yet should find, upon reflection, no warrant for so unlikely a charge. Again, the theory of two texts is inapplicable to this problem, at least in the sense it had in Luke: there the evidence was for two texts, but one author, while here there appear more authors than one. But one of the authors seems to be Luke. Well, and then? Did Luke perhaps interpolate or revise Mark? No, but he translated it, as the original Mark was in Aramaic, or had it translated for his own use, and then revised the translation. At a later time Luke's copy got into circulation and was again copied, and those copies went side by side with copies containing a translation made by somebody else, and our text contains a number of 'conflate' readings, which arose by the constant comparing and collating of the different copies. This seems to be, at least, a possible solution; but before adopting it, we must try to look more closely into the relations which may have existed between Luke and Mark.

That they knew each other is certain, and they lived together at some time in the company of Paul, and what one of them had written, could not remain unknown to the other. Moreover, it can hardly be questioned that Mark wrote his Gospel before Luke, and that this Gospel could not escape Luke's notice even before they came into personal contact; it follows, then, that Mark is one of Luke's authorities. Now, if this be so, it must become evident on comparing the two Gospels. They have been brought to that test long ago, and the result is, that Luke is rather generally regarded as depending, in a large measure, on Mark's authority. In the first place, the order of the narratives, as far as both authors have them in common, is almost invariably the same, and this argument is so much the stronger, as that order is either artificial or accidental, certainly not historical. There is on Mark the express testimony of Papias' presbyter : " Mark has not related things in their order, because he had not heard or followed the Lord, but had heard, at a later time, Peter, who delivered his teachings according to circumstances, and by no means as one who was making an orderly collection (σύνταξιν) of the Lord's sayings. So Mark is not to be blamed for writing some things as they came into his mind, his sole intention being to leave out nothing of what he had heard." If this was the origin of the order of events in Mark, it must be termed accidental, and as the same order is found in Luke, the reason cannot be that the same accidents happened twice, but that Luke borrowed from Mark. It has been suggested, it is true, that the order goes back to the relations of Peter and other evangelists, who by frequently relating the same things had at length established for them a fixed order ; but I do not think that this goes far enough to explain the constancy in

the sequence of so many narratives, which would not
be given in one sermon, but in a long series of sermons.
In the second place, the matter in Luke, as regards a
large number of narratives, is the same as in Mark,
only that the latter gives more detail; again and
again readers of Mark are struck by "autoptic
touches"[1] which are given by this narrator alone, and
for this reason one very soon finds it impossible to
derive Mark from Matthew or Luke, while the reverse
course lies wide open.   Also, the exclusively Galilaean
character of the history of our Lord, as given by the
three synoptic Gospels, seems to indicate a common
source, which may be found in Peter's sermons related
by Mark, for it is very natural that Peter, when
preaching in Jerusalem, did not generally tell what
had come to pass in the holy city itself, but what had
come to pass far away in Galilee.   But to prove the
hypothesis that Luke used Mark as his authority,
there is yet a third test, that of language, and that
test completely fails to give the expected result.   Verbal coincidences of any importance between Luke and
Mark are very rare even in the common text, and that
common text is, as we have seen, not very trustworthy
in particulars in the case of Luke, and very untrustworthy in the case of Mark.   I may give one instance:
on the calling of Levi the publican we read in Luke

[1] Salmon, Introduction (7th ed.), p. 138.

(v. 27 ff.): " He saw a publican, named Levi, sitting at
the receipt of custom : and He said unto him, Follow
me. And he left all, rose up, and followed Him."
Quite the same words, with the exception of the
" publican " and of " left all," are found in Mark
(ii. 14). But the words in Luke : " sitting at the
receipt of custom," are left out by the codex 700, and
upon reflection, we find that they are indeed rendered
superfluous by Luke's " publican "; likewise " rose up,"
which stands in close correspondence to " sitting," is
left out by the Sinaitic Syriac, and is likewise superfluous after Luke's " left all." In this way Luke's
text having been purified, the verbal coincidence with
Mark has vanished. On reading on in this story, we
find the substantial agreement of both evangelists to be
complete, but the verbal agreement to be almost totally
wanting. Even in the concluding sentence : " They
that are whole have no need of the physician," etc.,
Luke replaces Mark's (and Matthew's) ἰσχύοντες by
ὑγιαίνοντες.

You may say, of course, that even if Luke followed
the authority of our Greek Mark, he might nevertheless change ἰσχύοντες, which he never uses in this
sense, into ὑγιαίνοντες which he uses elsewhere, and
he alone of the evangelists. Besides, the difference
between Luke on the one side, and Matthew and
Mark (whose accounts have much in common) on the

other, does not merely consist in the choice of words, but also in the whole arrangement of the narrative; so Luke, even if he had another translation of Mark before him, must have allowed himself much liberty in its rendering. But the force of the argument consists in this, that while material agreement between the two extends over a rather large space, verbal agreement is never found in any considerable measure. And yet there is a great deal of such agreement not only between Mark and Matthew, but also between Luke and Matthew. Now we have seen in a former chapter (*see* on p. 175) that Matthew is not likely to have borrowed from Luke, but that more likely both of them used a common Greek authority. If this is true, it is proved that Luke did not shun verbal copying from a Greek source; and why then should he have declined to do so when Mark was this source? Was it because it was not quite good Greek, as for example where Mark has (x. 25): διὰ τῆς τρυμαλιᾶς τῆς ῥαφίδος? Why then did Luke (xviii. 25) write διὰ τρήματος βελόνης? Why, you may say, did Matthew (xix. 24, Tischend.) write τρυπήματος? It is perhaps difficult to answer, since nobody can tell which of these words was the common one in Palestine or elsewhere; but, as I have said, the strength of the argument lies in the constant occurrence of the observation, and not in any particular instance of

o

disagreement. That the observation is generally true, I have established elsewhere,[1] and may refer my readers to that place, if they do not choose to test the thing themselves, taking care, however, not to let themselves be deceived by assimilated readings.

I may now sum up my various arguments. Luke, in the first part of his Acts, followed an author who had written in Aramaic. Mark is very likely to be the author who first published these stories; he seems therefore to be Luke's Aramaic authority. If Mark's Acts were written in Aramaic, his Gospel originally was written in Aramaic also. Secondly, the textual condition of Mark's Gospel suggests the idea that there existed a plurality of versions of a common Aramaic original. But to speak more properly, we should perhaps say not versions but redactions. The discrepancies we found, *e.g.* in the beginning of Mark's 16th chapter, do not fall under the description of various Greek renderings for the same Aramaic words, and there are more cases like this. Among the various readings in Mark we recognized some as bearing distinctly the character of Lucan style, without being borrowed from Luke. Lastly, it appeared to us that the scarcity of verbal agreement between Luke and our Mark strongly dissuades us from the hypothesis of Luke's using this Mark; while,

[1] *See* my edition of Luke, p. xiv ff.

on the other hand, the material agreement is such as
to render a dependence of Luke on Mark even more
than probable. The conclusion to be drawn is this,
that Luke used another Mark. And now we may
go further and suggest that Luke, before writing
his own Gospel, made a Greek redaction of that of
Mark, not for his own use only, but also for that
of Christians speaking Greek. Another translation
of Mark, or other translations, were made by other
persons, and one version among these was that which
eventually predominated, but the others have at least
left their traces.[1]

Or is all this rather wild conjecturing? Is there
not a common and widely-spread opinion, that Mark
wrote for Romans, therefore, of course in Greek? I
ask, what are the proofs? Because he bears a Roman
name? No, but because there are Latin words in Mark,
such as κεντυρίων, instead of which the others employ
the Greek ἑκατόνταρχος. I say this is a vulgarism,

---

[1] Readings of Lucan character, besides those already mentioned,
are the following: iv. 19, καὶ αἱ περὶ τὰ λοιπὰ ἐπιθυμίαι, words
which are omitted by D etc. (ἐπιθυμία and ἐπιθυμεῖν, περί with
accusative, λοιπός, never in Mark, but all of them in Luke, cf.
Acts xix. 25, etc.); iii. 21, οἱ γραμματεῖς καὶ οἱ λοιποί, D, etc.,
see Luke xxiv. 9, etc. ; ibid. 22, οἱ ἀπὸ Ἱεροσολύμων καταβάντες
(instead of these words the Latin e has et ceteri, and D's reading
in 21 seems originally to belong to 22), cf. Acts xxv. 7 ; x.
24, τοὺς πεποιθότας ἐπὶ χρήμασιν (ACD etc.), see Luke xviii. 9 ; xiv.
58, ℵ gives ὅτι εἶπεν, c, k, hic dixit, instead of ἡμεῖς ἠκούσαμεν αὐτοῦ
λέγοντος ; with the latter cf. Acts vi. 11, 14.

not a Latinism. The Greek as well as the Aramaic language of daily intercourse had received many such words, and *centurio* is actually found in the Syriac version. Any writer who cared for good Greek would take the equivalent Greek word, but this so-called Mark did not care for style, and this you may see from the first page of the little book to the last.[1] But there is still another argument: the two mites (λεπτά) of the widow are explained to be of the same value as a Roman *quadrans* (κοδράντης; Mark xii. 42). The supposition seems to be, that Roman coins were not known outside of Rome, and yet there is the *denarius* in the four Gospels and in the Apocalypse, and the *as* (ἀσσάριον) in Matthew and Luke. But at all events Mark was not writing for Palestinian readers, who did not need an explanation of λεπτά. He was not translated for the use of such, I should say, for of course this addition comes from the translator. There is in Mark a much larger addition of the same kind, vii. 3 f., on the washings of the Jews, violently interrupting the construction, and of course not in the Aramaic original, and perhaps not even in the original translation, since it looks much like a

---

[1] An instance of stylistic refinement introduced by various readings is found in vi. 7, *e* D: καὶ προσκαλεσάμενος τοὺς δώδεκα ἀπέστειλεν αὐτοὺς ἀνὰ δύο (instead of δύο δύο, which is an Aramaism), δοὺς αὐτοῖς ἐξουσίαν τῶν πνευμάτων τῶν ἀκαθάρτων, παραγγείλας αὐτοῖς μηδὲν αἴρειν (instead of ἵνα . . . αἴρωσιν) εἰς τὴν ὁδόν.

scholion.   If the condition of the actual Mark is such as I think I have proved it to be, no individual passages can be brought forward which will have any weight against my hypothesis.   Another feature in the actual Mark are the Aramaic words : *talitha kumi,* v. 41, *ephphatha,* vii. 34, which I take for relics of the original, preserved by the translator.

On the other hand, if Luke—which must seem the most hazardous part of the whole hypothesis—had made something like a Greek translation of Mark before writing his own Gospel, and had set that Mark in circulation, we understand much more easily why there are so many omissions in Luke.   He might presuppose many things to be known to many, or most, of his readers, and as he was himself composing a Gospel on a much larger scale, introducing a great deal of fresh matter, he was well entitled to leave out some part of that already known, lest his book should grow to an immoderate size.   Much stress has been laid recently on the size of Luke's books, as having been somehow prescribed to him by a literary custom, or by the customary length of the papyrus-rolls he used, and it is a fact that both of his books are very nearly of the same size.[1]   I think that there is some truth in this ; of course the size of Luke's roll could not prevent him from giving in the

[1] *See* Arnold Ruegg in *Theol. Studien u. Kritiken,* 1896, p. 94 ff.

Roman copy the seven words which are left out there (*see* above, p. 138), but that reason among others might influence him in abridgments of greater importance. Comparing the last chapters of Mark and of Luke, we find the following important omissions in the latter. He does not tell of (*see* above on p. 179 ff.) the institution of our Lord's Supper, nor the anointing in Bethany (Mark xiv. 3 ff.), nor the discourses on the betrayer of Jesus (ibid. 18 ff.), except very briefly and in a general way (Luke xxii. 23), deflecting at once to another discourse which is not given by Mark. Next he omits all details of the trial before the Sanhedrin (Mark 55 ff.), giving only the final and decisive question. Also he omits the "Eloi, Eloi," etc. (Mark xv. 34), and the discourses made on it. He must, of course, make his own Gospel independent of the use of another Gospel side by side with it, and must give, therefore, all that was necessary or desirable for the understanding of the story, whether it was already extant in Mark or not; but he was not bound to give everything he knew. The same reasons may account for the largest omission we find when comparing the two Gospels, viz., that of the whole series of stories beginning with Mark vi. 45, and extending to viii. 13. There is in that part of Mark the story of the second feeding of the multitude, and Luke might easily dispense with giving that. But he actually leaps from the end of the story about the first feeding to the end of that about the second, leaving out all that comes between. This looks like a piece of carelessness in using his authorities, which, however, may be excused by the reflection that he did not feel bound to give all, nor would he deprive his readers of those stories which he did not give, there being a book within their reach where they might find them, the "Gospel according to Mark" (εὐαγγέλιον κατὰ Μᾶρκον), as the title would be.

I think that if we still possessed this form of Mark in its integrity, we should find there verbal agreement with Luke to a very large extent: *e.g.* we should find there "to preach *the gospel*," in iii. 14 (= Acts i. 2), as D gives (*see* above, p. 142), and the identical stories told in similar words. That passage in Mark iii. 14 ff. being of some importance, we shall allow it to detain us a little more.

The form A (Lucan) is there preserved for some length, differing greatly from B; the witnesses for A are, besides D, some old Latin versions: the Vercellensis *a*, the Palatinus *e*, the Colbertinus *c*, and others. Of course there is no want of conflated readings in D and elsewhere; but the purified text A appears to be this: (14) "And He ordained that twelve should be with Him, whom also He named apostles (= Luke vi. 13), (15) and gave them power that they might heal sicknesses, and cast out devils, and going about preach the gospel. (16) And Simon (*see* i. 16) He surnamed Peter; (17) but collectively He called them Baneregez, which is, The sons of thunder. They were these: Simon and Andrew, James and John (*see* i. 19), (18) and Philip, and Bartholomew, and Judas and Matthew, and Thomas and James, the son of Alphaeus, and Simon the Cananite (?), (19) and Judas Iscariot, who also betrayed Him." [1]

The names are identical with those in Luke, with one exception in the order ; the most important thing is that the name of Sons of Thunder is transferred to the whole body of the apostles, the thunder evidently being compared to their voice of preaching. For that same reason the preaching is mentioned after the heal-

---

[1] I give the two texts A and B in Greek (many peculiarities re maining doubtful) :

A.

(14) Καὶ ἐποίησεν ἵνα ὦσιν δώδεκα μετ᾽ αὐτοῦ, οὓς καὶ ἀποστόλους ὠνόμασεν (= L. vi. 13), (15) καὶ ἔδωκεν αὐτοῖς ἐξουσίαν θεραπεύειν τὰς νόσους καὶ ἐκβάλλειν τὰ δαιμόνια (cp. L. ix. 1), καὶ περιερχομένους κηρύσσειν τὸ εὐαγγέλιον. (16) καὶ ἐπέθηκεν (τῷ) Σίμωνι ὄνομα Πέτρον, (17) κοινῶς δ᾽ ἐκάλεσεν αὐτοὺς Βανηρεγέζ (700), ὃ ἐστιν υἱοὶ βροντῆς. ἦσαν δὲ οὗτοι Σίμων καὶ Ἀνδρέας, Ἰάκωβος καὶ Ἰωάνης κ.τ.λ.

B.

(14) [Καὶ ἐποίησεν δώδεκα] (to be cancelled, see ver. 16) ἵνα ὦσιν μετ᾽ αὐτοῦ, καὶ ἵνα ἀποστέλλῃ αὐτοὺς κηρύσσειν, (15) καὶ ἔχειν ἐξουσίαν [θεραπεύειν τὰς νόσους καὶ] (om.אB al.)ἐκβάλλειν τὰ δαιμόνια, (16) καὶ ἐποίησεν τοὺς δώδεκα (καὶ ...δ. om. AD al.), πρῶτον Σίμωνα, καὶ ἐπέθηκεν ὄνομα τῷ Σίμωνι Πέτρον, (17) καὶ Ἰάκωβον τὸν τοῦ Ζ. καὶ Ἰωάνην τὸν ἀδελφὸν αὐτοῦ, καὶ ἐπέθηκεν αὐτοῖς ὄνομα Βοανηργές, ὃ ἐστιν υἱοὶ βροντῆς᾽ (18) καὶ κ.τ.λ.

ing, that there might be a near connection between the preaching and the common name.

I think I have now said enough on this subject, as it is not my intention, nor ought it to be, to solve the so-called synoptic problem, but only to give such contributions for its solution as are afforded to me by textual criticism. Upon the whole I am afraid that textual criticism is apt to render the problem even more complex, since it tends to split a seeming unit, such as Mark's book, into a plurality of books; but this is, in my opinion, quite in accordance with the facts themselves. There was a time in the Latin Church, when, as Jerome states, there existed almost as many Latin versions of the Greek New Testament as there were copies,[1] each congregation having not only its own copy, but in that copy a separate version. Afterwards that plurality was gradually more and more reduced, and now the Roman Catholic Church has one authorized Vulgate. I think there was also a time in the old Christian Church when there existed almost as many Greek Gospels as there were Christian communities, not differing widely, perhaps, from each other in any individual case, but still not wholly identical. Afterwards a gradual reduction was effected, and now we are accustomed to

---

[1] Preface to the Gospels (*Tot enim sunt exemplaria paene quot codices*).

read only four Gospels, and each of them in one fixed form and text. But Papias' presbyter still knew more Matthews than one, and is it then astonishing that I try to establish that there were, and in some measure still are, two separate Lukes, and that in Mark the case is even more complicated? And, besides, all those many "predecessors of Luke" of whom he speaks existed, although, with the single exception of Mark, we are not even able to guess who they may have been.

CHAPTER XII.

TEXTUAL CONDITION OF JOHN'S GOSPEL.

THERE is but one Gospel now left for us to consider, that of John. The problems it presents are sufficient to fill up many books ; but I shall speak in the main of its textual condition, after having briefly discussed, or touched upon, some important general points.

There is a tradition recorded by a Latin manuscript of the ninth century, according to which Papias of Hierapolis, whom we mentioned just now, was the original copyist to whom John dictated his Gospel. Of course this cannot be true, but there seems to lie behind the corrupt tradition some fact which was really related by Papias. Now there is other testimony much like this, coming from a Greek compilation of commentaries (*catena*) on St. John, where the words are: John dictated his Gospel to his disciple, Papias Eubiotus of Hierapolis, in order to give a necessary supplement (πρὸς ἀναπλήρωσιν) to the information given by those who before him had preached the gospel to all the nations upon earth. This last clause reminds one of a passage in Eusebius (*Hist. Eccl.* iii. 24, 7), which is of this tenor : It is told (φασίν) that after the three other Gospels had already come into general notice, John, while approving their contents as authentic, said that he still missed in them the account of Christ's first doings, and that this was his reason for writing his own. Afterwards there comes in Eusebius the long passage on Papias, and the excerpts from him referring to Matthew and Mark ; as there are no excerpts given regarding John, we may infer that Eusebius did not find anything noteworthy in Papias that he had not already related. But the name of John's copyist would not seem to him very noteworthy, unless this copyist were Papias himself, so that this form of the tradition is disproved also by Eusebius' silence.

On the other hand the Catena, by presenting two names for that copyist, offers the easy explanation that in reality Papias had given the name of his own fellow-citizen Eubiotus as that of the copyist, a name which was blended by later ignorance with that of the author of the notice. For Eubiotus (Εὐβίοτος, wrongly spelt -ίωτος in the MS.) is a well-attested Greek name, and on the other hand it is as impossible to take it for a second name, or surname, of Papias, as to regard it as

an adjective. The adjective, of course, exists, but not
in common use, and it would require the article
before it ; a second name of Papias would also have
the article, like Δίων ὁ Κάσσιος, or Σαῦλος ὁ καὶ
Παῦλος.[1]

I earnestly hope that the day will come when
this conjecture will be brought to the test, by the
recovery of Papias' work, either in a Syrian or
Armenian translation, or even in the original Greek
form, although there is more hope for fragments
of that, from Oxyrhynchus or some other ruins of
an ancient town, than for an entire manuscript.
Meanwhile scientific theologians do well to retrench
themselves in new positions, since the old ones, by
that discovery, might become hopelessly untenable.
I am sure that we should find in Papias, among
much rubbish of worthless tradition, a good deal
of trustworthy information on John, I mean the
apostle and not the presbyter. It is true that
Eusebius found in Papias two Johns mentioned,
as in the catalogue of authorities given by Papias
and preserved by Eusebius the name of John comes
twice, first among those presbyters, that is apostles,
whose death occurred before his own time, and

---

[1] It would not be impossible that the words in the Latin MS.,
disscripsit vero evangelium dictante Johanne recte, are a blundering
translation of ἔγραψε δὲ τὸ εὐαγγ. ὑπαγορεύοντος Ἰωάνου Εὐβίοτος.

secondly, together with one Aristion, as one of those disciples of the Lord who in Papias' youth were still alive; Eusebius even affirms that he laid claim to having heard these himself, although in the quoted words of Papias, as they stand, this is not stated. He calls the second John by the same title which he had previously used for Peter and the other apostles, viz., presbyter or elder, and gives him that epithet in contradistinction to Aristion: "what Aristion and the presbyter John, the disciples of the Lord, relate"; evidently then this John must be the apostle or an apostle, if there were two. But there were not two, and so the passage appears to be utterly confused, unless we accept the conjecture recently proposed by the Greifswald Professor, Joh. Haussleiter, who strikes out the first mention of John, taking it for an interpolation which had crept into the text, before Eusebius' time, after the name of John's brother James, with which his was so frequently combined.[1] Haussleiter urges that the list is given by pairs: Andrew—Peter, Philip—Thomas, James—Matthew (if John is left out), and that Papias introduces the second, third, and fourth of these names by "or what" (*scil.* "have related"), while he drops the "what," leaving only the "or,"

---

[1] *Theolog. Literaturblatt*, xvii. Jahrgang, 1896, nr. 39. *See* also Provost Salmon's Introduction (7th ed.), p. 268 f.

before James and Matthew, as it was natural towards the end of an enumeration; now John's name comes in between these two with "or what," which is incongruous, and a clear trace of the interpolation.[1] If we adopt this emendation (as I am much inclined to do), it does not follow of course that the John who wrote the Apocalypse was identical with the apostle. For although Eusebius is not unwilling to ascribe that book to the "presbyter" John, we must be aware that Papias did not mention the Apocalypse,[2] and that its author never styles himself "presbyter," nor apostle, but simply "John," which indeed does not go very far as a proof of identity. But the author of the second and third Johannine epistles styles himself "presbyter"; this then must be the apostle, and why not?[3] Moreover, the traditions introduced

[1] The Greek words are: Εἰ δέ που καὶ παρηκολουθηκώς τις τοῖς πρεσβυτέροις ἔλθοι, τοὺς τῶν πρεσβυτέρων ἀνέκρινον λόγους· τί Ἀνδρέας ἢ τί Πέτρος εἶπεν ἢ τί Φίλιππος ἢ τί Θωμᾶς ἢ Ἰάκωβυς ἢ τί Ἰωάνης ἢ Ματθαῖος ἤ τις ἕτερος τῶν τοῦ κυρίου μαθητῶν, ἢ τί Ἀριστίων καὶ ὁ πρεσβύτερος Ἰω., οἱ τοῦ κυρίου μαθηταί, λέγουσιν (this present tense refers, of course, to the time of which Papias is narrating, and not to the time when he wrote).

[2] I do not feel bound to credit Andrew of Caesarea (a writer of the end of the fifth century), who adduces Papias among many other witnesses for the authenticity of the Apocalypse. If there had been in Papias a mention of that book, we should read it in Eusebius, who expressly states that Justin cited the Apocal. (iv. 18, 8), and Theophilus of Antioch (iv. 24), and Apollonius (v. 18, 14).

[3] See Salmon, l. c., p. 270 ff.

by Papias with the formula, " This said the presbyter,"
must be referred to John the apostle, as *e.g.* that
about Mark's Gospel. I say again : Why not ? And
just so that about those vines of the Millennium, which
will have each ten thousand branches, and each branch
ten thousand twigs, and each twig ten thousand
bunches, and each bunch ten thousand grapes, and
each grape will produce twenty-five barrels of wine ;
for Irenaeus, who gives this quotation, expressly introduces it by the words, " as those Elders (Papias, etc.),
who had seen John the disciple of the Lord, relate,
that they heard from him, how the Lord taught about
those times, and said " ; then follow the words, and
after them Papias' written authority is adduced.
Why, this is mere rubbish, and cannot have been
taught by our Lord, or related by His disciple. I
fully agree with this criticism ; let us hope, then,
that when Papias comes to light, the formula, " This
said the presbyter," will not be found at the head
of this apocryphal teaching, although the words of
Irenaeus rather point to the opposite conclusion.

We see therefore that this is doubtful ground, and
hence the great divergencies between different scholars.
Whilst in Professor Haussleiter's eyes the " presbyter "
John is dead and buried, in those of Professor Harnack
he is, on the contrary, full of vigorous life ; Harnack
does not shrink from assigning to him, and not to

the apostle (who may have been, however, his teacher
and authority), the authorship of the Johannine writings and especially of the Gospel.[1]   He insists chiefly
upon one passage of the Gospel, which gives, in his
opinion, the clear proof that the narrator and composer cannot be the eye-witness, but must be a different
person.   There are in xix. 35 f. the words: "And
he that saw it bare record ($\mu\epsilon\mu\alpha\rho\tau\acute{\nu}\rho\eta\kappa\epsilon\nu$), and his
record is true : and he ($\dot{\epsilon}\kappa\epsilon\hat{\iota}\nu\text{o}\varsigma$) knoweth that he saith
true, that ye might believe.   For these things were
done, that the scripture should be fulfilled," etc.
There are, it is true, different interpretations given
of these words, and there are different readings also,
and more than that.   Professor Harnack says: "It
would be quite unwarranted to regard the ver. 35
as an interpolation."   Indeed ? He ought to be
aware that a very good warrant, the Latin *e*, and
besides an ancient MS. of the Latin Vulgate, omit the
ver. 35, *e* giving in ver. 36 $\delta\acute{\epsilon}$ instead of $\gamma\acute{\alpha}\rho$; for
$\delta\acute{\epsilon}$ there are even more witnesses, and among these
Nonnus in his metrical paraphrase of the Gospel, who
renders besides in ver. 35 the text: "He that saw
it bare record, and of him ($\dot{\epsilon}\kappa\epsilon\acute{\iota}\nu\text{o}\nu$) we know that

---

[1] Harnack, *Chronologie der altchristl. Litteratur*, i. 659 ff. Harnack
does even more than this. He makes his "John the Presbyter"
establish the canon of our four Gospels, including his own, and
impose that canon on the whole Church.

P

the record is true."[1]　This Nonnus was a gifted poet,
an Egyptian by birth, who lived about the beginning
of the fifth century, and wrote besides and before this
paraphrase a voluminous epic poem called Διονυσιακά.
In his paraphrase he is, of course, continually amplify-
ing, but he takes great care not to omit any word of
the sacred text.　Now, the passage in question reminds
one of the first epilogue to the Gospel in xx. 30 f.:
" But these (signs) are written, that ye might believe,"
etc., and of the second epilogue too, xxi. 24: " This
is the disciple which testifies (μαρτυρῶν) of these
things, and wrote these things, and we know that
his testimony is true," the last clause " and we,"
etc., being omitted by Nonnus.　Moreover, there
is to be compared v. 32 (in Christ's words): " There
is another that beareth witness (μαρτυρῶν) of me;
and I know that the witness which He witnesseth
of me is true," and in the Third Epistle of John
(of the authenticity of which I have no doubt), ver.
12 : " Demetrius hath good report (Δημητρίῳ μεμαρ-
τύρηται) of all men, and of the truth itself:　yea,
and we also bear record (μαρτυροῦμεν) ; and ye know
(οἶδας) that our record is true."　There is therefore
not the least doubt of the Johannine character of

---

[1] Nonnus' words are : ἀνὴρ δ' ὅστις ὄπωπεν ἑῷ πιστώσατο μύθῳ μαρ-
τυρίην ἀτίνακτον· ἀριστονόοιο δὲ κείνου ἴδμεν ὅτι ζαθέη καὶ ἐτήτυμος ἔπλετο
φωνή· ταῦτα δὲ πάντα πέλεσκεν κ.τ.λ.

the words in xix. 35, but we may question the
genuineness of the last clause, on Nonnus' authority,
as it may have crept in from the passage in xx. 31,
and likewise question, on the same authority, the
genuineness of "and we know," etc., in xxi. 24; for
that too may be an amplification due to xix. 35.
There is a difficulty removed in this way, for how
can a distinction be made between the author and
writer (ὁ γράψας) of the narrative and the person
or persons narrating (ἡμεῖς)?   But the same difficulty
is, on the same authority, translated into xix. 35,
where Nonnus gives "we know" instead of "he
knows."   The case there is, that an endless discussion
has been carried on about the ἐκεῖνος, the question
being, whether that pronoun may be employed of
the author himself.   It is rather hard to affirm
this, and Zahn's view, who refers the pronoun to
Jesus, whilst it seems to be recommended by the
grammar, appears very strange from another point
of view.   On the other hand, Nonnus' reading is,
as far as this sentence goes, quite unexception-
able; only there is again the distinction between
the author and the "we."   Well, then, the whole
verse on the authority of e must be relegated from
the text to the margin, the γὰρ in ver. 36 being
of course replaced by δέ.   If we accept this, we
have to state that John's text has been commented

upon at a very ancient time by some disciples of his, who copied his style; for the Johannine style, as we have seen, is evidently there.

We may now leave this special question, in order to take a general view of the condition of St. John's text. Are there more instances of interpolation, or of commenting upon a text, or whatever we may call it? If we are to regard as spurious, or at least dubious, all those particles which have not an universal and unanimous attestation, there is indeed a very great deal of dubious matter in John. This is even in some measure a recognized fact, certain passages having been cancelled by recent editors upon the evidence of the Alexandrian MSS. which omit them. The most conspicuous instance is in chap. v., where some words in ver. 3 and the whole of ver. 4 are now left out, on the authority of the best MSS. (among which B and D). There can indeed be no doubt that the ver. 4 does not come from John, since the style is wholly different,[1] quite apart from all considerations with regard to the contents: "For an angel went down (but according to the Alexandrinus A ' bathed,' ἐλούετο), at a certain season into (in) the pool, and troubled the water: whosoever then first after the troubling of the

---

[1] There is nowhere in the N.T. ᾧ δήποτε or οἵῳ δηποτοῦν, nor κατέχεσθαι νοσήματι, except in D, Luke iv. 38, κατέχ. πυρετῷ, nor νόσημα itself.

water stepped in was made whole of whatsoever disease
he had." But the impotent man says to Jesus in ver.
7: " Sir, I have no man, when the water is troubled, to
put me into the pool : but while I am coming, another
steppeth down before me." This is the universal
reading there, except that one MS. adds " and receives
healing," and another, " and I walk away in my in-
firmity." After the removal of ver. 4, it is evident
that ver. 7 has become unintelligible. Turning to
Nonnus, we find in him no trace of ver. 3 or 4, but
instead of these he must have read something like
this : " where a sick man, as soon as he saw the water
being troubled spontaneously, bathed and was made
whole." I am sure that if we had a text like this,
no offence could be taken : if we suppose the pool
(κολυμβήθρα) to have been rather narrow, there would
be no room for more than one man at a time, and
Nonnus indeed uses throughout the word ἀσάμινθος,
" bathing-tub," and, as we have seen, the singular of the
man. There is then in this passage not interpolation
only, but the genuine text has been replaced by a
spurious comment, of course at a very ancient time.
For even those witnesses who omit the comment, indirectly show that it had existed in one of their
archetypes, where it had been cancelled upon better
authority, but without giving the genuine words exhibited by that authority. Or else the narrative given

by John had been from the beginning incomplete in this respect, and was afterwards supplemented by others in different ways. You see there is the same quicksand as in Mark. Going on in this narrative we find more of it: ver. 9, "and on that same day was the Sabbath"; but D and *e* (Nonnus) simply: "And it was the Sabbath"; ver. 10, "The Jews therefore said unto him that was cured," but *e* without "unto . . . cured," and the verb employed here for "cured" does not exist elsewhere in John; "It is the Sabbath day"; but this is not in Nonnus, or in the Sinaitic Syriac; "it is not lawful for thee to carry thy bed"; but Nonnus: "who had bid him," etc., in close agreement with ver. 11, where he renders this text: "And he answered them: He that has made me whole, the same told me to take up and walk." Conversely in ver. 12: "Then asked they him (*e*, 'the Jews asked him, saying'): What man is that which said unto thee, Take up thy bed, and walk?" Nonnus not only preserves the direct form of speech (which is replaced by the indirect in א both here and in 11), but also the words, "thy bed," which are left out by אB and others. Ver. 13: "And he that was healed wist not who it was." Instead of ὁ ἰαθεὶς, cf. iv. 47, there are these various readings: ὁ δὲ ἀσθενῶν, ὁ δὲ τεθεραπευμένος, καὶ ὁ ἄνθρωπος (Syr. Sinait., and apparently Nonnus), ὁ δὲ (*q*). "For Jesus had conveyed Himself away, a multitude being in that place." The whole sentence is left out by Nonnus, and the verb employed here (ἐκνεύειν) is wholly foreign to the New Testament. And was this a reason for the man's not knowing Jesus? Perhaps not, but if Jesus had remained there the Jews would have recognized Him. On the other hand, we do not even question whether Jesus was there or not, if the sentence is left out; for the place where the Jews met with the man who was carrying his bed was, of course, not Bethesda, where the narrator has left Jesus.

Take another narrative, you will find the same uncertainty of readings, and now and then a manifest gloss, or interpolation. In chap. iv. 6 ff., the two Syriac MSS., those of Cureton and of Mrs. Lewis, make a transposition of ver. 8 into ver. 6: "Jesus therefore, being wearied, sat thus on the well; (ver. 8) for His disciples were gone away into the city to buy meat. (6) And as Jesus sat (there) it was about the sixth hour, (7) and a woman cometh," etc. We have seen on a former occasion (p. 56 ff.) a very good transposition given by the Sinaitic Syriac; in the present case both collocations of the sentences seem to be equally possible. In the next verse (9): "Then saith the woman of Samaria unto Him, How is it that Thou, being a Jew, askest drink of me, which am a woman of Samaria? for the Jews have no dealings with the Samaritans" (οὐ γὰρ συγχρῶνται Ἰουδαῖοι

Σαμαρίταις), the last clause is left out by אD, etc., and here again the interpolation is evident, as συγχρῆσθαί τινι is foreign to New Testament Greek. But also γυναικὸς Σαμαρίτιδος οὔσης is superfluous, and is left out by the Sinaitic Syriac. It is, however, worth noticing that in the following discourse, as in other discourses and speeches of Jesus, omissions are much rarer. In ver. 14 *e* and Nonnus present a shorter form : "And whosoever drinketh of the water that I shall give him shall never thirst; but there shall be in him a well of water springing up," etc. I do not think that the sentence loses anything by this omission, as the words omitted ("the water that I shall give him ") are already there in the former part.

Now, how are we to explain this condition of St. John's text ? In the first place, we must define that condition more exactly, and in contra-distinction to that in Mark as well as to that in Luke. Is there something like a double text ? By no means; for the witnesses for the longer and for the shorter form are continually changing places; for instance *c*, which often bore testimony to an omission of words, is in other places a witness for some enlargement. Moreover, there are passages where all our witnesses give a more or less prolix text, but in quite different ways. In ii. 2 there are these readings: "And when they wanted wine "; or, "And they had no wine, because the wine of the marriage festival had been spent"; or (e) "And it came to pass, that because of the great multitude of guests the wine was spent." None of these readings commends itself by particular Johannine words; on the contrary, we may object to each of them from this point of view, and what if we leave to John nothing of all this? The narrative will be somewhat short, it is true, but will not cease to be intelligible to everybody. So, the thing we find does not look like a double form of text, but, as I stated before, like an uncommented text on the one side (not always preserved), and a text accompanied with different comments on the other. This is not the case, as we have seen, in Mark, or in Luke, where the clauses omitted by D are sometimes very characteristic and always in accordance with Luke's style, while in John there is now and then a striking difference between comments and text. Again, we did not find anything in John which reminded us by its style of another individual writer, as was the case in Mark.

Well, then, if this is the condition we actually have before us, let us seek for an hypothetical explanation which may suit it. The copyists of our MSS. and of their archetypes are either to be condemned all alike, or to be absolved all alike; as the former is impossible we shall do the latter. Then there remains only this hypothesis. The archetype of St. John's Gospel,

written by Eubiotus, or by some one else, whoever
he may have been, and destined in the first place for
John's disciples who lived with him and for the
Christian community in which he lived, was very soon
copied for the use of distant disciples and communities;
and the copyists being themselves disciples, took the
liberty of enlarging the text here and there, of course
each in a different way, and this was the origin
of most variants.   Whether the angel bathing in the
pool (v. 4) was added by a disciple of John, I am not
certain; but so much is evident, that a man of "very
little understanding," like Papias (who is so charac-
terized by Eusebius), was quite capable of commenting
in this way.   On the other hand, xix. 35, which
also did not seem to us to be a part of the original
text, shows both understanding and familiarity with
John's style; there must have been disciples of all
kinds, and so there are comments of all kinds.

Among individual passages of contested reading
there is none more deserving our attention than the
thirteenth verse of the first chapter: "Which were
born, not of blood, nor of the will of the flesh, nor of
the will of man, but of God."   And yet very few of
my readers, as I should think, are aware that there is
any difference of reading here.   But if we slight the
variants found in our MSS. and versions (e.g. that
"which" is left out in D and others, being replaced in

English, of course, by "they"), we cannot slight the
evidence given by a witness of such antiquity and such
high standing as Tertullian, whose copy of John not
only did not contain the relative pronoun, but also had
"he was born" instead of "(they) were born." He
goes so far as to ascribe the other reading, "they
were born" (ἐγεννήθησαν), which he found with his
adversaries the Valentinians (but without the pronoun
"which"), to their wilfully changing the text. If Tertullian is not sufficient, there is Irenaeus also attesting
the same reading—obscurely, it is true, as to the
omission of the pronoun, but very distinctly as to the
singular and to the reference to Christ—not to speak
of authors so *late* as Ambrose and Augustine. Is this
not enough? There is Justin, too (*Dialog.* ch. 63),
with a rather unmistakable allusion. You find the
whole case stated in the large work of Dr. Resch, who
has the great merit of calling attention to this highly
important "variant," and decides in favour of it.[1] But
let us judge, with all impartiality and fairness, on careful consideration, both of the external and of the
internal reasons. There are four readings: "He was
born," "who was born" (*qui natus est*, the Latin *b*, a
Verona MS. of the fourth or fifth century), "they
were born," and "who were born." The two readings
with the pronoun are suspicious, even for the reason

[1] A. Resch, *Aussercanonische Paralleltexte*, iv. 57 ff.

that there are others without it; for copyists were
very apt to add pronouns and conjunctions, as they
have done a thousand times in John and elsewhere;
on the other hand, there is no apparent reason why
the pronoun should have been left out. That John's
style is asyndetic you will recognize at once,
wherever you open his book; in this same proem
you have the conjunction only before vers. 5, 12
(where D and *e*, and Tertullian and Cyprian leave
it out), 14, 16, 17, while it is missing in 2, 3, 4,
etc. But if we leave out the pronoun here the case
will be decided; for "they were born not of blood
. . ., but of God, *and* the Word was made flesh, and
dwelt among us," etc., is manifestly impossible. So,
if you will maintain the ordinary reading, you must
needs return to the "who," which still *might* be left
out accidentally. But even with the pronoun you
have the "*and*" in 14 much against you: why are
these two sentences connected, although the former
refers to the time after Christ's appearance, and the
latter goes back to the appearance itself and at the
same time to the "Word" of vers. 1-3 ? There is a
manifest break in the series of ideas in ver. 14, and
here the author, after having spoken mostly in dis-
connected sentences, puts in the "and."

But, you may say "he was born" must refer to the
Word, or to the Light, and with one of these subjects

the sentence becomes absurd. I deny the necessity : look at the words immediately preceding: "But as many as received Him, to them gave He power to become the sons of God, to them that believe on His name." On whose name ? On that of the Word, or of the Light ? Of course not, but on the name of Jesus Christ. Well, then you have there the subject for ver. 13. There is still more to be said against the ordinary reading. "Sons of God" in 12 evidently bears a spiritual meaning, and cannot be understood otherwise; why then this strong assertion that these spiritual sons are not born of blood, *nor* of the will of the flesh, *nor* of the will of man, but of God ? Of course, the reader must say ; for this is indeed self-evident. Give back to the sentence its reference to Christ, and the strong assertion is justified. But why has this reference been destroyed by "were born" (ἐγεννήθησαν) ? Not by malice, as Tertullian suggests, but by mere inadvertence : "was born of God" was assimilated to the preceding. "to become the *sons* of God." Afterwards the pronoun came in, either in the singular or in the plural, because a sentence like this : "Not of blood, nor of the will of the flesh, nor of the will of man, but of God He was born," with its subject not indicated until as late as in the fifteenth Greek word, was somewhat harsh and seemed to require the elucidation which was given by the pronoun.

There is a very well-known passage in ii. (ver. 4), where Jesus says to His mother: "Woman, what have I to do with thee? mine hour is not yet come." The Greek words are τί ἐμοὶ καὶ σοί, γύναι; οὔπω ἥκει ἡ ὥρα μου. This "what have I to do with thee?" or literally, "what is there (in common) to me and you?" does not cease to vex readers, whatever may be said in explanation of it, for the phrase used is the same which the demons use in speaking to Jesus (see e.g. Matt. viii. 29), and which is frequent both in the Old Testament and in colloquial Greek of the time, quite in the meaning of our "Let me alone." But Nonnus, in his paraphrasing of the words, makes a very slight alteration, which wholly changes the sense: instead of "and" (καὶ) he has "or" (ἤ),[1] and now this sense comes out: What is that to me, or to you? (cf. Paul, 1 Cor. v. 12). Namely, that they have no wine does not concern you at all, and it does not concern me yet: for mine hour is not yet come. I am sure most readers will be of my opinion and prefer ἤ to καὶ, although there is but one witness for the former, and

---

[1] Τί ἐμοί, γύναι, ἠὲ σοὶ αὐτῇ; In case anybody should conjecture ἠδὲ instead of ἠὲ, I notice that the index of words given in Scheindler's edition of Nonnus does not contain ἠδὲ at all; besides the αὐτῇ is evidently incompatible with that alteration. By the way, I can state by means of the same index, that N. renders ἤ instead of καὶ also in viii. 14 (ἢ ποῦ; so BD, etc.), x. 10 f. (ἢ θύσῃ ἢ ἀπολέσῃ . . . ἢ περισσὸν); xii. 38 (ἢ ὁ βραχίων), 49 (ἢ τί λαλήσω, as d and the Coptic version), whether rightly or not, I do not decide.

that quite an obscure one.   It is much to be regretted, that in this chapter we are destitute of the aid of the Sinaitic Syrian, which, as my readers will remember, afforded us excellent help for xviii., where we found a very clear instance of inverted order (*see* above on page 56 ff.).   This too seems to be a special feature in the textual condition of John ; carelessness in copying, and the leaving out of sentences, which were afterwards supplied in the margin, and from thence came again into the text, but at a wrong place, may have been the early causes of this damage.   It seems to have taken place now and then even on a larger scale : Prof. H. Wendt[1] has proposed a highly probable conjecture on vii. 15-24, which he removes from their present place, putting them at the end of v.

But as I am dealing strictly with MSS. evidence, I prefer to give another instance which is no less clear, although not of so great importance.   Read attentively xxi. 7 f.: " Now when Simon Peter heard that it was the Lord, he girt his fisher's coat unto him (for he was naked), and did cast himself into the sea.   And the other disciples came in a little ship, for they were not far from land, but as it were two hundred cubits."   Why, if they had

---

[1] H. Wendt, *Die Lehre Jesu,* i. 228 ff.: cf. also Bertling, in *Studien u. Kritiken,* 1880, 351 ff. (before Wendt), and F. Spitta, *Zur Geschichte und Litter. des Urchristenthums,* 199 ff. (after W.).

been very *far* from land they would much more
naturally have come in the ship, and not swimming.
Turn now to our Syriac witness from Sinai, which
gives this quite clear and coherent text: "... he
girt his fisher's coat unto him (the words 'for he
was naked' are left out) and did cast himself[1] into
the sea, and came swimming (Nonnus too renders
this clause), for they were not far from land ('but
. . . cubits' is left out).   But the other," etc.
There can be no doubt that this is the right order,[2]
but you may be still wondering why it was inverted,
and what is to become of the words "for he was
naked," and of "but . . . cubits," and of the "and
came swimming."   Of course it is impossible here to
know anything certainly: we may imagine an *original*
text having some authentic supplements in the margin
(as is very frequently the case with our own manuscripts), and shall be able to explain by that hypothesis
the omissions (the supplements having been overlooked
by a copyist), either wholly or in part, and the wrong
order (the copyist having corrected his mistake, but
in a wrong way), and all we want to explain.   At
any rate, the "but as it were two hundred cubits"
looks rather authentic, and the "for he was naked"

---

[1] Ἔβαλεν ἑαυτὸν common text, but D ἥλατο, and so Nonnus.

[2] In Nonnus the clause "for they," etc., stands after σύροντες . . .
ἰχθύων, at the end of ver. 8.

(*i.e.* he had no undergarment on) seems to be indis-
pensable, while "came swimming" may be a comment
made on the model of "the other disciples came in
a ship." Thus you leave much uncertainty, you will
say. Of course I do; am I that Indian Bird (*see*
above on page 79) possessing the miraculous gift of
discerning, in any given case, between spurious and
genuine particles? We may be able to do so in
some cases, and more easily when the object of our
doubts is of some extent; but there are only too
many things about which we cannot ourselves arrive
at a firm conviction, still less convince others.

Having spoken quite enough of variants and of
minute matters, I shall conclude with some remarks
on the words in v. 2: "Now there is at Jerusalem
by the sheep *market* (rather *gate*; the Greek text
has only ἐπὶ τῇ προβατικῇ) a pool, which is called
in the Hebrew tongue Bethesda,[1] having five porches."
"There *is*"? Then Jerusalem was still existing at
the time when this was written; and even John's
Gospel, the latest of all, was written before the year
71. I am not at all afraid of this inference which
has actually been drawn, and before our century;
but as it is of great importance, we must be very
cautious. There is a German pastor, O. Wuttig,
who has recently published a book on this Gos-

----

[1] "Which . . . Bethesda" is missing in Nonnus.

pel,[1] trying to establish that it was written in Judaea, and before any other Gospel, in spite not only of common opinion, but also of tradition, since Eusebius, and perhaps even Papias, nay even Papias' presbyter, that is John the apostle, regarded it as being destined to give supplements to other Gospels. Of course I cannot enter into this subject here; but the objections to Wuttig's thesis seem to be very serious. He too relies very much on the "is" in v. 2, although it evidently does not go far enough for him: I at least am quite convinced that in the year 68, that of Nero's death, both Mark and Luke were in existence and generally known. But what he says on the "is" in question is very judicious: he attaches to that present the more importance, as John ordinarily uses the imperfect even when speaking of localities (see iv. 6, "Now Jacob's well was there"), and as this was and is quite a common assimilation to the tense of the narrative, not at all implying that the thing in question has now ceased to exist. But if we use the present tense amid the imperfects of our narrative, we certainly imply that this is even now so. Moreover, there is no passage in this Gospel where the destruction of Jerusalem is alluded to, and the latest event mentioned,

---

[1] Licent. O. Wuttig, *Das Johanneische Evang. und seine Abfassungszeit*, Leipzig (G. Böhme), 1897.

the martyrdom of Peter, is universally placed in Nero's time. Nevertheless, if you are to suspend a hundred-weight, you must take a rope and not a thread. If the "is" ($\check{\epsilon}\sigma\tau\iota\nu$) is universally attested, there are so many threads joining that they will form a rope; if not, I shall call the thing still a thread, and have no mind to suspend the hundred-weight by it. Now, which is the case? Greek MSS. are concordant for "is," but Nonnus has $\hat{\eta}\nu$, "was," and so have all the Syriac versions, and the Armenian, and the two old Egyptian versions. Still the evidence for "is" is far stronger, as Nonnus does not count much here, his stand-point being rather that of his own time, and the "was" might be due to assimilation to the "was" of the preceding verse; as an editor, I should certainly give "$\check{\epsilon}\sigma\tau\iota\nu$," and not $\hat{\eta}\nu$. But that is not the question here. The threads do not make up the rope, and so I leave this question like many others to my readers.

INDICES.

I. TO PERSONS, SUBJECTS, AND GREEK WORDS.

II. TO PASSAGES OF THE N.T. DISCUSSED.

ADDENDUM to pp. 70 f. and 106 f.

Licent. E. von der Goltz, of Berlin, recently discovered, in a monastery at Mount Athos, a manuscript of the Acts and Epistles, not very ancient, it is true, but, at all events, derived from an ancient and very valuable original. The margin contains numerous scholia, in which many variants, especially in the Pauline Epistles, are traced back to quotations by Eusebius, Origen, Irenaeus, and Clement; there is exhibited a degree of carefulness even about small things, which we were by no means prepared to meet with. But, at the same time, it is quite evident that there existed no authoritative text of the sacred books. In the Acts there is one important addition of D, which is acknowledged both in the text and in a scholium: ch. XV., 20 and 29, the words καὶ ὅσα ἂν μὴ θέλωσιν αὐτοῖς γενέσθαι, ἑτέροις μὴ ποιεῖν (after τοῦ αἵματος in v. 20 and after πορνείας in v. 29) stand in the text included by asterisks (*), much in the same way as in the Syrus posterior of Acts (see p. 109), or in the remnants of Origen's *Hexapla*. The scholium attests that this was the reading given by Irenaeus in his third book, and by Eusebius in his sixth and seventh book against Porphyrius. Another scholium (to v. 29) gives the close of the Epistle of the Apostles according to Irenaeus: ἐξ ὧν διατηροῦντες ἑαυτοὺς εὖ πράξετε, φερόμενοι ἐν ἁγίῳ πνεύματι (without ἔρρωσθε), stating, at the same time, that καὶ τοῦ πνικτοῦ in v. 20 and καὶ πνικτῶν in v. 29 was omitted by the same authority. We actually find this very text (= D) in the extant Latin version of Irenaeus. Now it becomes more and more impossible to ignore Western variations, since it is proved that they go back to such very early times, and that attention was bestowed upon them by the ancient Greek Church itself. My own larger edition of the Acts is nothing but an expansion of the method followed by the Athous in those passages of ch. XV., and I should think that there were Greek manuscripts where the same method was thoroughly followed, as it is in the Syrus posterior. Lic. v. d. G. is preparing a publication of the scholia; meanwhile he has kindly allowed me to state so much here.